THE NEW CAMBRIDGE SHAKESPEARE

GENERAL EDITOR
Philip Brockbank, *Director, The Shakespeare Institute, University of Bi*

ASSOCIATE GENERAL EDITORS
Brian Gibbons, *Professor of English Literature, University of*
Robin Hood, *Senior Lecturer in English, University of York*

THE COMEDY OF ERRORS

THE NEW CAMBRIDGE SHAKESPEARE

THE COMEDY OF ERRORS

Edited by

T. S. DORSCH

Emeritus Professor of English,
University of Durham

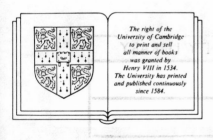

The right of the
University of Cambridge
to print and sell
all manner of books
was granted by
Henry VIII in 1534.
The University has printed
and published continuously
since 1584.

CAMBRIDGE UNIVERSITY PRESS

Cambridge
New York   New Rochelle   Melbourne   Sydney

Published by the Press Syndicate of the University of Cambridge
The Pitt Building, Trumpington Street, Cambridge CB2 1RP
32 East 57th Street, New York, NY 10022, USA
10 Stamford Road, Oakleigh, Melbourne 3166, Australia

First published 1988

Printed in Great Britain at
the University Press, Cambridge

British Library cataloguing in publication data
Shakespeare, William
The comedy of errors. – (The New Cambridge Shakespeare).
I. Title   II. Dorsch, T.S.
822.3'3   PR2804.A2

Library of Congress cataloguing in publication data
Shakespeare, William, 1564–1616.
The comedy of errors / edited by T. S. Dorsch.
p.   cm. – (The New Cambridge Shakespeare)
Bibliography: p.
ISBN 0 521 22153 6.   ISBN 0 521 29368 5 (pbk.)
I. Dorsch, T.S.   II. Title   III. Series: Shakespeare, William, 1564-1616.
Works. 1984. Cambridge University Press.
PR2804. A2D67   1988
822.3'3 – dc19   87-23299 CIP

ISBN 0 521 22153 6 hard covers
ISBN 0 521 29368 5 paperback

THE NEW CAMBRIDGE SHAKESPEARE

The *New Cambridge Shakespeare* succeeds *The New Shakespeare* which began publication in 1921 under the general editorship of Sir Arthur Quiller-Couch and John Dover Wilson, and was completed in the 1960s, with the assistance of G. I. Duthie, Alice Walker, Peter Ure and J. C. Maxwell. *The New Shakespeare* itself followed upon *The Cambridge Shakespeare*, 1863–6, edited by W. G. Clark, J. Glover and W. A. Wright.

The New Shakespeare won high esteem both for its scholarship and for its design, but shifts of critical taste and insight, recent Shakespearean research, and a changing sense of what is important in our understanding of the plays, have made it necessary to re-edit and redesign, not merely to revise, the series.

The *New Cambridge Shakespeare* aims to be of value to a new generation of playgoers and readers who wish to enjoy fuller access to Shakespeare's poetic and dramatic art. While offering ample academic guidance, it reflects current critical interests and is more attentive than some earlier editions have been to the realisation of the plays on the stage, and to their social and cultural settings. The text of each play has been freshly edited, with textual data made available to those users who wish to know why and how one published text differs from another. Although modernised, the edition conserves forms that appear to be expressive and characteristically Shakespearean, and it does not attempt to disguise the fact that the plays were written in a language other than that of our own time.

Illustrations are usually integrated into the critical and historical discussion of the play and include some reconstructions of early performances by C. Walter Hodges. Some editors have also made use of the advice and experience of Maurice Daniels, for many years a member of the Royal Shakespeare Company.

Each volume is addressed to the needs and problems of a particular text, and each therefore differs in style and emphasis from others in the series.

PHILIP BROCKBANK
General Editor

CONTENTS

ILLUSTRATIONS

Illustrations 2, 3, 9, 10, 11, 12 and 13 are reproduced by permission of the Shakespeare
Birthplace Trust, Stratford-upon-Avon

PREFACE

We all learn from those who came before us. How can an editor of today adequately express his indebtedness to the prodigious labours of such scholars as Chambers, Greg, and Bullough? I hope that, when I have drawn upon the work of earlier editors and critics, I have never neglected to acknowledge my debt.

Of recent editions of *The Comedy of Errors* I have found most helpful those of Quiller-Couch (the New Shakespeare), R. A. Foakes (the Arden Shakespeare), Stanley Wells (the New Penguin Shakespeare), and G. Blakemore Evans (the *Riverside Shakespeare*).

I must give special thanks to Professor John W. Velz, of the University of Texas at Austin, with whom I have discussed aspects of the play. Mrs E. E. Morse, of Dove Cottage, read my introduction in manuscript and suggested some improvements. My son Alan Dorsch provided some helpful historical material. I owe much to students in universities in England, Australia, Germany, and America with whom I have, in tutorials and seminars, dissected the play; even more to colleagues in these universities who have put their knowledge of Shakespeare at my service.

I am grateful to Dr Levi Fox and his colleagues in the Shakespeare Birthplace Trust at Stratford-upon-Avon; to the Joe Cocks Studio, also of Stratford; to Miss Elisabeth A. Jocz of the Thomas Fisher Rare Book Library in the University of Toronto; to Dr Marcello Gallucci of the University of L'Aquila; to Mrs Thom, Librarian of Gray's Inn; and to the New York Public Library: these persons and institutions have supplied, or helped me to procure, the illustrations with which this volume is embellished. Mr C. G. Harlow, of Westfield College, kindly gave me photo-copies, from his own copy of the 1591 edition of the Bishops' Bible, of passages to which the play owes much of its character. Mr C. Walter Hodges has discussed with me the kinds of stage that might have been used for the performance of 1594, has put forward an alternative to my own views, and has provided three admirable sketches.

I must also express my gratitude to Mrs K. Stenhouse, of the Department of French at Durham, and to Mrs Sue Jones, of Dove Nest, Windermere, who have triumphed over my difficult handwriting and produced an elegant typescript for the press. Miss Sarah Stanton, Miss Janet Coombes, and Mr Paul Chipchase, of the Cambridge University Press, have given me invaluable help in the shaping of this volume, especially Mr Chipchase as my copy-editor. They too have earned my warm thanks.

My greatest debt is to Philip Brockbank, in whom I, as a contributor to the series, have found everything that could be desired in a General Editor.

T.S.D.

ABBREVIATIONS AND CONVENTIONS

The abbreviated titles of Shakespeare's plays are those of the *Harvard Concordance*, a few of them modified by the General Editors. Other editions of Shakespeare are abbreviated under the editor's surname (Malone, Rann) unless they are the work of more than one editor. In such cases an abbreviated series name is used (NS, Var. 1778). Except where it has been necessary to quote from the Folio, quotations and line-references throughout this edition are from *The Riverside Shakespeare*, edited by G. Blakemore Evans, 1974, on which the *Harvard Concordance* is based.

1. Shakespeare's plays

Ado	*Much Ado about Nothing*
Ant.	*Antony and Cleopatra*
AWW	*All's Well That Ends Well*
AYLI	*As You Like It*
Cor.	*Coriolanus*
Cym.	*Cymbeline*
Err.	*The Comedy of Errors*
Ham.	*Hamlet*
1H4	*The First Part of King Henry the Fourth*
2H4	*The Second Part of King Henry the Fourth*
H5	*King Henry the Fifth*
1H6	*The First Part of King Henry the Sixth*
2H6	*The Second Part of King Henry the Sixth*
3H6	*The Third Part of King Henry the Sixth*
H8	*King Henry the Eighth*
JC	*Julius Caesar*
John	*King John*
LLL	*Love's Labour's Lost*
Lear	*King Lear*
Mac.	*Macbeth*
MM	*Measure for Measure*
MND	*A Midsummer Night's Dream*
MV	*The Merchant of Venice*
Oth.	*Othello*
Per.	*Pericles*
R2	*King Richard the Second*
R3	*King Richard the Third*
Rom.	*Romeo and Juliet*
Shr.	*The Taming of the Shrew*
STM	*Sir Thomas More*
Temp.	*The Tempest*
TGV	*The Two Gentlemen of Verona*
Tim.	*Timon of Athens*
Tit.	*Titus Andronicus*

TN	*Twelfth Night*
TNK	*The Two Noble Kinsmen*
Tro.	*Troilus and Cressida*
Wiv.	*The Merry Wives of Windsor*
WT	*The Winter's Tale*

2. Editions and references

Abbott	E. A. Abbott, *A Shakespearian Grammar: An Attempt to Illustrate Some of the Differences between Elizabethan and Modern English*, 3rd edn, revised, 1876 (reference is to numbered paragraphs)
Alexander	*William Shakespeare, The Complete Works*, ed. Peter Alexander, 1951
Baldwin	*The Comedy of Errors*, ed. T. W. Baldwin, 1928 (Heath's American Arden Shakespeare)
Barton	Anne Barton, introduction to *The Comedy of Errors* in *The Riverside Shakespeare*, 1974
Brooks	Harold Brooks, 'Themes and structures in *The Comedy of Errors*', in *Early Shakespeare* (Stratford-upon-Avon Studies, 3), 1961
Bullough, *Sources*	Geoffrey Bullough (ed.), *Narrative and Dramatic Sources of Shakespeare*, 8 vols., 1957–75
Cam.	*The Works of William Shakespeare*, ed. W. G. Clark, J. Glover, and W. A. Wright, 1863–6 (Cambridge Shakespeare)
Capell	*Mr William Shakespeare his Comedies, Histories, and Tragedies*, ed. Edward Capell, 1768
Chamber Accounts	See E. K. Chambers, *The Elizabethan Stage*, 4 vols., 1923
Chambers, *Allusion-Book*	*The Shakespeare Allusion-Book*, re-ed. E. K. Chambers, 1932
Chambers, *WS*	E. K. Chambers, *William Shakespeare: A Study of Facts and Problems*, 2 vols., 1930
Child	Harold Child, 'The stage-history of *The Comedy of Errors*', NS, pp. 115–19
Coleridge	*Coleridge's Writings on Shakespeare*, ed. Terence Hawkes, 1959
Collier	*The Works of William Shakespeare*, ed. John Payne Collier, 1842–4
conj.	conjecture
Cuningham	*The Comedy of Errors*, ed. Henry Cuningham (Arden Shakespeare)
DNB	*The Dictionary of National Biography*
Dowden	Edward Dowden, *Shakspere: A Critical Study of His Mind and Art*, 8th edn, 1886
Dyce	*The Works of William Shakespeare*, ed. Alexander Dyce, 1857
F	*Mr William Shakespeares Comedies, Histories, & Tragedies*, 1623 (First Folio)
F2	*Mr William Shakespeares Comedies, Histories, & Tragedies*, 1632 (Second Folio)
F3	*Mr William Shakespeares Comedies, Histories, & Tragedies*, 1664 (Third Folio)
F4	*Mr William Shakespeares Comedies, Histories, & Tragedies*, 1685 (Fourth Folio)
Ff	The four Folios
Foakes	*The Comedy of Errors*, ed. R. A. Foakes, 1962 (Arden Shakespeare)
Greg, *Gesta*	*Gesta Grayorum: or the History of the High and Mighty Prince Henry, Prince of Purpoole . . . who Reigned and Died, A.D. 1594*, ed. W. W. Greg (Malone Soc. Reprints)

Greg, *SF*	W. W. Greg, *The Shakespeare First Folio: Its Bibliographical and Textual History*, 1955
Halliwell	*The Complete Works of William Shakespeare*, ed. James O. Halliwell, 1853–65
Hanmer	*The Works of Shakespear*, ed. Thomas Hanmer, 1744
Harvard Concordance	*The Harvard Concordance to Shakespeare*, comp. Marvin Spevack, 1973
Hogan	C. B. Hogan, *Shakespeare in the Theatre, 1701–1800*, 2 vols., 1952
Johnson	*The Plays of William Shakespeare*, ed. Samuel Johnson, 1765
Keightley	*The Plays of William Shakespeare*, ed. Thomas Keightley, 1864
Kittredge	*The Complete Works of Shakespeare*, ed. G. L. Kittredge, 1936, rev. Irving Ribner, 1971 (*The Kittredge Players Edition . . .*, 1958, has many photographs of productions)
Malone	*The Plays and Poems of William Shakespeare*, ed. Edmond Malone, 1790
Muir	Kenneth Muir, *Shakespeare's Sources*, I: *Comedies and Tragedies*, 1957
Nashe	*The Works of Thomas Nashe*, ed. R. B. McKerrow, 5 vols., 1904–10
NS	*The Comedy of Errors*, ed. Sir Arthur Quiller-Couch and John Dover Wilson, 1922
Noble	Richmond Noble, *Shakespeare's Biblical Knowledge*, 1935
Odell	G. C. D. Odell, *Shakespeare from Betterton to Irving*, 2 vols., 1920
OED	*The Oxford English Dictionary*
Onions	C. T. Onions, *A Shakespeare Glossary*, rev. edn, 1919
Pelican	*The Comedy of Errors*, ed. Paul A. Jorgensen, in *William Shakespeare: The Complete Works*, ed. Alfred Harbage, 1956, revised edn, 1969 (Pelican Shakespeare)
Pope	*The Works of Shakespear*, ed. Alexander Pope, 1723–5
Rann	*The Dramatic Works of Shakespeare*, ed. Joseph Rann, 1786–94
Riverside	G. Blakemore Evans (ed.), *The Riverside Shakespeare*, 1974
Rouse	*The Menaechmi: The Original of Shakespeare's "Comedy of Errors": The Latin Text together with the Elizabethan Translation*, ed. W. H. D. Rouse, n.d.
Rowe	*The Works of Mr William Shakespear*, ed. Nicholas Rowe, 1709
Rowe²	*The Works of Mr William Shakespear*, ed. Nicholas Rowe, 2nd edn, 1709
SD	stage direction
SH	speech heading
Singer	*The Dramatic Works of William Shakespeare*, ed. S. W. Singer, 1826
Sisson	C. J. Sisson, *New Readings in Shakespeare*, 2 vols., 1956
Stationers' Register	*A Transcript of the Registers of the Company of Stationers, 1554–1640*, ed. Edward Arber, 5 vols., 1875–94
Staunton	*The Plays of William Shakespeare*, ed. Howard Staunton, 1858–60
Steevens	*The Plays of William Shakespeare*, ed. Samuel Johnson and George Steevens, 1773
subst.	substantively
Theobald	*The Works of Shakespeare*, ed. Lewis Theobald, 1733
Thirlby	Christopher Spencer and John Velz, 'Styan Thirlby: a forgotten "editor" of Shakespeare', *Shakespeare Studies* 6 (1970), 327–33
Tilley	*A Dictionary of the Proverbs in England in the Sixteenth and Seventeenth Centuries*, 1950
Var. 1778	*The Plays of William Shakespeare*, with the corrections and additions of various commentators, to which are added notes by Samuel Johnson and George Steevens, 1778

Walker	William S. Walker, *A Critical Examination of the Text of Shakespeare*, 1860
Warburton	*The Works of Shakespeare*, ed. William Warburton, 1747
Wells	*The Comedy of Errors*, ed. Stanley Wells, 1972 (New Penguin Shakespeare)
Wilson	F. P. Wilson, *The Plague in Shakespeare's London*, 1927

Biblical quotations are taken from the Bishops' Bible, 2nd edn, 1591

The Great Hall of Gray's Inn from the east end

INTRODUCTION

Date of composition

There can be no doubt that *The Comedy of Errors* is one of Shakespeare's earliest plays, but the year of its composition remains uncertain. Its first recorded performance took place on 28 December 1594, and it has been argued that it was written in this year;[1] but there are other indications, both within the play and from parallels with other works, that Shakespeare wrote it earlier, and it is now generally accepted that the date must be moved back to the first years of the 1590s.

Passages in support of this occur in the dialogue in which Dromio of Syracuse describes to his master the physical attributes (relating them to various countries) of the fat kitchen wench who, mistaking him for his twin, claims him as her lover. First:

ANTIPHOLUS S. Where France?
DROMIO S. In her forehead, armed and reverted, making war against her heir.   (3.2.109–11)

This seems to be a reference to the civil war in France, usually ascribed to the years 1589–93, between the Catholic League and Henry of Navarre, who in 1589 had been named as heir to the throne by Henry III of France who was murdered by a fanatical monk after joining forces with the Huguenots against the League. Fighting had occurred earlier than 1589 and continued beyond 1593, but was fiercest between these years. In April 1591 Queen Elizabeth sent forces under Sir John Norris to support Navarre, and about the same time the Earl of Essex also took troops to France for this purpose.[2] Whatever the earlier or later history of the strife, peace – or a firm truce – was established in July 1593, and Navarre, converted to Catholicism, was accepted as Henri Quatre, King of France. W. W. Greg[3] claimed that 'the jest about France . . . "making warre against her heire" would have had no point except between the summer of 1589 and that of 1593, when Henry IV was at war with the League'. We may perhaps go further and suggest that in 1591 especially, when the English expeditions went to France, there would have been much talk and speculation about the events taking place in that country, and that, if *The Comedy of Errors* was written near this time, the lines quoted would have been seen by the first audience as an allusion to those events. A few moments later in the dialogue:

ANTIPHOLUS S. Where Spain?
DROMIO S. Faith, I saw it not, but I felt it hot in her breath.

---

[1] By, for example, Sidney Thomas, 'The date of *The Comedy of Errors*', *SQ* (1956), 377–84. Thomas notes, *inter alia*, resemblances in versification to that of the narrative poems, and feels that a Plautine play containing legal language might well have been written for a Gray's Inn audience.
[2] Norris took 3,000 men to Brittany, Essex 4,000 to Normandy, although the Queen reluctantly granted him his commission for France only on 21 July 1591. See *DNB* under Norris and Devereux.
[3] Greg, *SF*, p. 200.

ANTIPHOLUS S. Where America, the Indies?

DROMIO S. O, sir, upon her nose, all o'er embellished with rubies, carbuncles, sapphires, declining their rich aspect to the hot breath of Spain, who sent whole armadoes of carracks to be ballast at her nose.

(3.2.116–22)

Quiller-Couch[1] was undoubtedly right in suggesting that these lines reflect the jubilation of the English over the defeat of the Spanish Armada in 1588: 'In 1591 (say) our great national deliverance from the Armada would yet prevail in memory, to win applause' – that is, as an event from the past. The two passages strengthen the belief that the play belongs to the very early 1590s.

No other lines, as far as we know today, can be said with such apparent authority to embody topical allusions. No outside references to *Errors* have been found earlier than the record of its performance at the end of 1594. There was a severe outbreak of plague between June 1592 and the autumn of 1593, with only a short intermission in midwinter. The theatres were closed and the acting companies went on tour.[2] The people of London would have been preoccupied with fear for their lives and sorrow for their losses, and the more responsible would have had imposed on them heavy duties regarding safety and sanitation;[3] they would have had little time to reflect or write about plays they had seen before they were afflicted. For other pointers towards the date of *Errors*, its relationship to contemporary writings, especially other plays of Shakespeare, must be taken into account.

We get only a little help, in fact, from the work of Shakespeare's contemporaries. In a note to 4.4.83–4 of *Errors* Quiller-Couch (NS, p. 107) draws attention to a close parallel with a passage in Nashe's *Foure Letters Confuted* (?1592, 1593), a retort to and attack on Gabriel Harvey. Denying that he has brought money to redeem his master from 'Tartar limbo', Dromio of Ephesus exclaims (in the Folio text):

> Monie by me? Heart and good will you might,
> But surely Master not a ragge of Monie.
>
> (4.4.79–80)

The passage in Nashe reads, 'heart and good will, but never a ragge of money'.[4] The parallel gives no help towards the dating of *Errors*. Although there can be no certainty, it is just as likely that Nashe took the words from Shakespeare as the other way round, or they may have been a commonplace of the period. In his mockery of Harvey Nashe had earlier in *Foure Letters Confuted* quoted from *The Spanish Tragedy* and gone on to say: '*Memorandum*: I borrowed this sentence out of a Play. The Theatre, Poets hall, hath many more such prouerbes' (Nashe, I, 271–2). It is probable enough that in the present parallel he was borrowing from such a proverb – or from Shakespeare. We must not infer too much from apparent echoes that could move either way between *Errors* and Marlowe's *Edward II* – the question 'What, will you murder me?' is found in both plays, and the singeing of Pinch's beard and its quenching in 'puddled mire' resembles the shaving of King Edward's beard and his standing in 'mire and puddle' (*Edward II* 5.3.36, 5.5.56). The first that we hear precisely about the date of *Edward II* is that it was entered in the Stationers' Register on 6 July 1593, and, although it must have been written earlier, we do not know when. Other ambiguous echoes in the anonymous *Arden of*

---

[1] NS, pp. x–xi.   [2] Chambers, *WS*, I, 27–46.   [3] Wilson, pp. 14–84.   [4] Nashe, I, 301.

Feversham carry us no further, for again its earliest history begins for us with its entry in the Register on 3 April 1592.[1] These parallels do no more than confirm an early date for *Errors*.

Comparisons with other plays by Shakespeare are more helpful. *The Comedy of Errors*, *The Taming of the Shrew*, and *The Two Gentlemen of Verona* are sometimes, on grounds of style, comparative sophistication, and shared elements of classical influence and reference, grouped together as being almost certainly Shakespeare's earliest comedies (with *Love's Labour's Lost* as a probable fourth).[2] All three have much (often decorative) 'Lylyan' verse in regular iambic lines; all have comic interchanges between masters and servants; all are influenced by works with a classical background. (The *Henry VI* plays, generally dated between 1590 and 1592, show a similarly limited flexibility in their versification.)

The closest affinities, for action and characters, lie between *Errors* and *The Taming of the Shrew*. Both plays devise farcical settings for the expression of Pauline principles requiring a wife to subjugate herself to her husband – principles expressed in *Errors* by Luciana and (less directly) by the Abbess, and in *The Shrew* by Katherina in her final speech. There are specifically parallel situations too. Antipholus of Ephesus is denied entry into his house because indoors his twin is being entertained as the husband of his own wife Adriana, and in *The Shrew* Vincentio is barred from a house in which the Merchant and Tranio are masquerading as Vincentio himself and as Lucentio; the Merchant in *The Shrew* is deceived into thinking that as a Mantuan he is under threat of death in Padua, just as Egeon, a Syracusan, is actually under threat of death in Ephesus. In each play there are several comic scenes between masters and servants: the Dromios are berated for their unwitting mistakes; Grumio has his ears wrung for pretending to misunderstand Petruchio; and Lucentio's boy Biondello is beaten by Vincentio for pretending not to know him. In his confusion at being addressed by Adriana as her husband, Antipholus of Syracuse exclaims:

What, was I married to her in my dream?
Or sleep I now, and think I hear all this?   (2.2.173–4)

In the same way Christopher Sly is confused when he is 'transformed' into a noble lord and given a noble lady for wife, and exclaims:

Am I a lord, and have I such a lady?
Or do I dream? Or have I dreamed till now?   (Ind. 2, 68–9)

Identical wording is found in one pair of stage directions in the Folio texts:

Exeunt omnes, as fast as may be, frighted.   (*Err.*4.4.140)

Exit Biondello, Tranio and Pedant as fast as may be.   (*Shr.*5.1.111)

[1] For the dates supplied for *Edward II* and *Arden of Feversham*, see *The Revels History of Drama in English*, III, 1975, pp. 63–4.
[2] *LLL* has the court of Navarre as its setting; the entry of the King and the lords disguised as Russians (5.2.158 ff.) may be an echo of a similar embassy of Russians during the Gray's Inn Revels of Christmas 1594, though it is more likely that the echo was the other way round. Navarre and his concerns would have been of interest for some time during and after the war in France.

A further, structural, parallel needs fuller presentation. It is more than likely that the comic action of both plays, not merely that of *Errors*, was originally enclosed within a frame. The opening scene of *Errors* presents Egeon's account of the loss of his wife, one of his sons, and that son's slave; Egeon then disappears until at the end he is reunited with his whole family. *The Taming of the Shrew* opens with two inductions in which Sly is tricked into thinking he is a nobleman who is to be entertained with a play. In the Folio text, and hence in modern editions and performances, we hear no more of him. But was this Shakespeare's intention? On 11 June 1594 Henslowe recorded a performance of a play entitled 'the tamyng of A shrowe'; there is no reason to think that this was other than a play '. . . called the Tamyng of a Shrowe' entered in the Stationers' Register on 2 May 1594 and published in the same year as *The Taming of a Shrew*. In *A Shrew* (as it is called to differentiate it from Shakespeare's *The Shrew*) Sly is duped in two opening scenes – just as in *The Shrew*. He reappears four times: at Scene v, 187–94, and Scene xvi, 45–54, he comments on the play he is seeing and demands drink; at Scene xvi, 129–33, after the stage direction *Slie sleeps*, he is carried out, and is absent until after Kate has declared her complete subordination to her husband; he is brought back in his own clothes for the final episode (Scene xix), where he is awakened from 'the bravest dreame' and revealed as the drunkard of the opening.[1] The framework, like that of *Errors*, is complete. *A Shrew*, once regarded as the source, is now thought to be either a reconstructed text of *The Shrew* (a 'bad quarto'), or another derivative from the same original.[2] The evidence allows us to believe that Shakespeare wrote *The Taming of the Shrew* as a play in which the taming of Katherina was enclosed within a frame similar to that of *A Shrew*, that at some time his company used a curtailed version in which Sly was banished after the inductions (perhaps, with a reduced number of actors on tour, to play another part), and that this was the version printed in the Folio.

These many parallels are significant in that they show almost to a certainty that *Errors* and *The Shrew* were written within a short time of each other, and that Shakespeare, having written one of them, recalled from it characters and episodes, even a phrase, when he was writing the other. H. J. Oliver[3] thinks that *The Shrew* 'cannot be later, in its original Shakespearean form, than 1592'; Ann Thompson[4] leaves us 'free to suppose that it was written in or about 1590'. Neither claims priority for the one or the other play.

Links with the third play of the trio are more tenuous. Comparisons have been drawn between Launce's 'Cate-log' of the 'condition' of his mistress (*TGV* 3.1) and Dromio's description of the 'kitchen vestal', but there is no close similarity. R. A. Foakes[5] finds resemblances in the use in the two plays of phrases, jests, and 'relatively unusual words' (only relatively unusual); it is difficult to see affinities other than in the regularity of the 'early' versification.

---

[1] The scene-divisions and line-references are from Bullough's reprint of *A Shrew* (*Sources*, 1, 69–108). The corresponding references in F. S. Boas's Shakespeare Classics reprint of 1908 are 1.324–31, 4.2.45–53 and 124–33, Epilogue.

[2] See H. J. Oliver (ed.), *The Taming of the Shrew*, 1984, pp. 15–29; Ann Thompson (ed.), *The Taming of the Shrew*, 1984, pp. 164–74.

[3] Oliver (ed.), *Shr.*, p. 32.

[4] Thompson (ed.), *Shr.*, p. 9.   [5] Foakes, pp. xxii–xxiii.

Guidance towards the date of *The Comedy of Errors* can perhaps be gained from earlier writers. Quiller-Couch finally settled for 'the date 1591–2 generally assigned to this play'. Chambers[1] summarised evidence that might support various dates, and gave his preference for either the spring or the December of 1592. T. W. Baldwin, the most prolific writer on the play, argued[2] that it was written in about December 1589. He saw references to the hanging (which he believed Shakespeare saw) of a priest named Hartley in 1589; to the Armada; to *Tamburlaine* (entered in the Stationers' Register on 14 August 1590, but probably written in about 1588); to Lyly's *Mother Bombie* (Stationers' Register, 18 June 1594, perhaps written in about 1587), where the name Dromio occurs; and to the French wars. His evidence has not been found convincing.

In *Shakespeare's Life and Art* (1939) Peter Alexander suggested a date between 1584 and 1589 (pp. 67–9), but in his *Shakespeare* (1964) he modified this view. He noted (p. 81) associations between the work of Marlowe and Kyd, the three parts of *Henry VI*, *Titus Andronicus*, *The Shrew*, and an early version of *Hamlet* – plays which he thought were written during Shakespeare's 'connexion with Pembroke's men in the years immediately preceding the plague of 1592–4'. While still holding (p. 116) that 'there is nothing in *The Comedy of Errors* to rule out a date before 1589 and much to support it', he found elements in this and other early plays by Shakespeare that 'may point to their production in this period [before the plague] – presumably 1591, or at the earliest 1590'.

Greg[3] confined himself to the years 1589–93. Geoffrey Bullough[4] referred to 1594 as a possibility, 'but verbal resemblances in Nashe and *Arden of Feversham* suggest an earlier date, perhaps 1592. There is some likeness in theme and style to *The Taming of the Shrew*.' Foakes[5] granted reasons for dating the play in 1589, 1591–3, or 1594, but 'none of the evidence is very reliable'. Its links with other works and some internal evidence inclined him to think that it was written 'not long before or immediately after the long spell of plague which caused all acting to be prohibited in London throughout most of the year 1593, and which may have turned Shakespeare to writing his narrative poems'. E. A. J. Honigmann[6] assigns *Errors* to 1589, *The Shrew* to the preceding year; it is not relevant to his purpose to give supporting evidence for these dates. There is substantial agreement that *Errors* was written a good deal earlier than the performance at Gray's Inn at the very end of 1594.

It is possible, I think, to be more positive. Stanley Wells has argued convincingly[7] that *The Two Gentlemen* is the earliest of this group of comedies. I believe, from its greater swiftness and sharpness, and the perfect timing of its very complex plot, that *Errors* was written later than both *The Two Gentlemen* and *The Shrew*.[8] As E. M. W. Tillyard observed,[9] *Errors* resembles the *Henry VI* and *Richard III* plays in its elaborate and

---

[1] Chambers, *WS*, I, 311.
[2] Baldwin developed his thesis most fully in *William Shakspere Adapts a Hanging*, 1931. He also wrote at length on the date in *On the Compositional Genetics of 'The Comedy of Errors'*, 1965, pp. 18–36.
[3] Greg, *SF*, p. 200.   [4] Bullough, *Sources*, I, 3.   [5] Foakes, pp. xvi–xxiii.
[6] *Shakespeare: The 'Lost Years'*, 1985, p. 128.
[7] Stanley Wells, 'The failure of *The Two Gentlemen of Verona*', *Shakespeare Jahrbuch* (Heidelberg), 99 (1963), 161–73.
[8] Compare Marco Mincoff, 'The dating of *The Taming of the Shrew*', *English Studies*, 54 (1973), 554–65.
[9] E. M. W. Tillyard, *Shakespeare's History Plays*, 1944, pp. 135–9, 175, 199.

highly-wrought structure. I accept Ann Thompson's reasoned conjecture that *The Shrew* was probably written in 1590. The evidence and near-evidence strongly suggest that *The Comedy of Errors* was written between April 1591, when the English expeditions went to France and an allusion to the Armada could still have awakened proud memories in an English audience, and June 1592 when the plague, never far away, again became a serious menace to the people of London. Whether early or late within these limits cannot, I think, be decided, but I would guess from the topical allusions that it was in the summer or autumn of 1591. I suspect that it was written to be played for the first time before a legal audience (see pp. 19–20 below).

Sources

We now recognise that Shakespeare used multiple sources for his plays; a wide and retentive reader, he often read or recalled several versions of a tale to which he wanted to give his own dramatic form. Kenneth Muir has shown[1] that for the Pyramus and Thisbe episodes in *A Midsummer Night's Dream* he used his knowledge of at least half a dozen versions of the legend, from Ovid down to a poem of the 1590s; Bullough for the whole play prints[2] eight probable or possible sources and refers to other likely influences. A similar blending of sources is seen in *The Two Gentlemen*, a play nearer in date to *The Comedy of Errors*. For this Bullough provides[3] six sources or parallels (including Spanish, Italian, and German works, not all necessarily known to Shakespeare or read in the originals), and mentions others; he sees *The Two Gentlemen* as 'a dramatic laboratory in which Shakespeare experimented with many of the ideas and devices which were to be his stock-in-trade and delight for many years to come'. This could be said of other early comedies, *The Taming of the Shrew* or *Love's Labour's Lost*. The histories show the same diversity in their origins – several chronicles and earlier verse and drama. Invariably, too, Shakespeare drew on his reading, from his schooldays onwards, in a variety of tongues, and on the great fund of knowledge and ideas which formed the intellectual background of his age.

The sources of *The Comedy of Errors* are threefold in their nature: classical, represented by two or perhaps three of Plautus's plays; romantic – such tales as that of Apollonius of Tyre told by John Gower, and similar stories in later prose romances; and biblical, chiefly from the Acts of the Apostles and St Paul's Epistle to the Ephesians. Diverse and apparently incompatible as these traditions are, Shakespeare has synthesised them into a play with a consistent moral vision and theatrical style.

Plautus was in Renaissance Europe the most popular of the ancient playwrights. From the late fifteenth century onwards his plays were endlessly translated and adapted in Italy, France, Spain, and Germany.[4] Rodrigo Borgia, at that time Pope Alexander VI, had the *Menaechmi* played at the marriage of his daughter Lucrezia to Alfonso d'Este, and later, in 1548, Ippolito d'Este, Cardinal of Ferrara, entertained Henry II of France

---

[1] Muir, pp. 31–44. [2] Bullough, *Sources*, I, 367–422. [3] Bullough, *Sources*, I, 203–66.
[4] Many of these versions are noted by Gilbert Highet in *The Classical Tradition*, 1949.

and Catherine de Medici at Lyons with an Italian prose adaption of the same play. The *Menaechmi* was always a special favourite.[1]

The popularity of Plautus was as great in England as on the Continent. He was well known in places of learning, and Henry VIII had two of his plays performed for the French ambassador. *Thersites* (1537, perhaps by Nicholas Udall) and Udall's *Roister Doister* (?1552) owe much to the *Miles Gloriosus*, and the anonymous *Jack Juggler*, also of the 1550s, is adapted from the *Amphitruo* and precedes Shakespeare in its use of a husband denied entry into his own house. *Gammer Gurton's Needle*, probably written in the same decade, shows English folk in an English rustic setting, but is essentially Plautine.

Two lost plays sound of special interest: 'The historie of Error' acted by the 'children of Powles' (St Paul's) at Hampton Court on New Year's Day 1576–7, and 'A historie of Fferrar', acted by Sussex's Men in 1583. However, it cannot be known whether Shakespeare was indebted to either, and they are no more than possible sources; we can only guess that the *Menaechmi* may have lain behind them. (It is possible that in the second the form 'Fferrar' is a variant of the city-name Ferrara.)

Shakespeare knew Plautus well. From the *Mostellaria* he took the names of Grumio and Tranio in *The Shrew*, giving Tranio something of the function and spirit of his namesake. He knew others of the plays. The *Menaechmi* was his primary source for *The Comedy of Errors*.

This play presents the identical twin sons of a merchant of Syracuse of whom the elder, Menaechmus, was as a child lost to his father at a festival in Tarentum; in memory of the missing boy the younger, Sosicles, was given his name. When he grew up Sosicles–Menaechmus set off in search of his twin, and after six years arrived at Epidamnus, where the twin was living. In a number of comic episodes he encountered his brother's mistress (and her cook), wife, and father-in-law, and was accepted by all as that brother. He was in his confused state of mind thought to be insane, but by mistake the original Menaechmus was locked up as a madman. Finally, in a general confrontation, the perplexities were brought to an end.

Shakespeare retained the essentials of this plot – the identical twins with the same name, the arrival of the one in the city where the other was living, the same kinds of bewildering encounters (but in greater profusion), the seizure of the apparently mad man, and the solution of all the puzzles in a family reunion. So far he was faithful to his text.

However, he made many changes. He altered the names of his characters and added new characters – Egeon, the Duke, Luciana, the Abbess, Balthasar, Angelo, and, most important of all, the second Dromio. He moved the setting from Epidamnus to Ephesus, one of the most considerable city-ports in Asia Minor, famous for its temple and cult of Artemis (Diana), and well known from the Bible for its curious arts and evil spirits. He turned the courtesan from a major to a minor figure, and did not allow the visiting twin to make love to her. Where Menaechmus stole a cloak and a bracelet from his wife to give to

---

[1] In his Shakespeare Classics parallel-text edition of the *Menaechmi* and Warner's free translation of 1595 W. H. D. Rouse lists about a dozen European versions.

his mistress, Antipholus of Ephesus took, or intended to take, only a chain. The cook was not used, though he may have suggested the kitchen-maid. Finally, Shakespeare introduced pathos, suspense, beauty, and a love-interest into what he had taken up as a heartless farce.

Although he changed the place of action, he gave his Ephesus some of the character of the city described in the *Menaechmi* by the slave Messenio:

In Epidamnus you'll find the worst womanising and pub-crawling types, and the city's thick with the ghastliest swindlers and con-men. And then the whores – there's no place in the world can show you sweeter tarts. It's just because of this that the town's called Epidamnus – just because no one that comes here gets away without getting into a mess [*sine damno*].[1]

Knowing the biblical Ephesus, Shakespeare modified this description in Antipholus's much less indecorous lines at the end of his first act.

We find in some entry directions what seem to be Shakespeare's reminiscences of the Latin. In the Folio Antipholus of Ephesus is on one occasion introduced as 'Sereptus', recalling from Plautus's prologue *puerum surruptum* (38), *subruptust* (40), two similar forms later in the prologue (58, 60), and two in the prefixed *Argumentum*, all variant forms derived from *surripere/subripere*, and in the first three or four pages dinned in often enough to be remembered; Shakespeare's 'Sereptus' (? = *surreptus*) would mean 'snatched away', as Menaechmus was in his seventh year and Antipholus in infancy. Antipholus of Syracuse is once brought in as 'Erotes', once as 'Errotis'. These names could have come from *errare* (Sosicles and Antipholus both wander far), perhaps in some such form as *erraticus*; this form does not occur in Plautus, but Shakespeare might have remembered it from Ovid or Cicero. Less credible is the derivation, sometimes suggested, from Erotium, the name of Plautus's courtesan; or from Eros (genitive *Erotis*) – though Antipholus is a lover, he can scarcely be called erotic.

The *Menaechmi* is much shorter than most Elizabethan plays. In order to amplify it and to make it more fun, Shakespeare 'contaminated' it by adding episodes he found in another of Plautus's most highly regarded plays, the *Amphitruo* (even so *Errors*, with its 1,857 lines, is the shortest of Shakespeare's plays). It was from the *Amphitruo* that he adopted the idea of the twin slaves, although in the Plautus neither the masters nor the slaves were twins. The equivalent of Antipholus of Syracuse was Jupiter, taking the shape of Amphitruo, while Mercury impersonated Amphitruo's slave Sosia. Shakespeare always improved on his originals; by turning the Dromios into identical twins serving twin masters, he increased beyond measure the opportunities for confusion and error, increased too, with the reunion of a second pair of twins, the happiness at the end of the play. Also from this Roman play came the device of the husband denied entry into his own house. Jupiter masqueraded as Amphitruo in order to fornicate with Alcmena while Mercury as Sosia barred the door against her husband. Shakespeare refined the scene by attributing Antipholus of Ephesus's visit to the Porpentine with his wife's chain, not to a wish to be with his mistress, but to spite at being excluded, and he admitted no suggestion of adultery.

Shakespeare almost certainly read *Menaechmi* in Latin. The first English translation of

---

[1] *Menaechmi* 258–64. My translation is, in a modern idiom, faithful.

the play (a free rendering) was published by William Warner in 1595; it is possible that Shakespeare saw it in manuscript, but not likely, for there are not the many verbal echoes or parallels that we expect when he was recalling an earlier work; the use by both writers of such words as 'stale', 'patch', and 'harlot' means nothing, since Shakespeare often used these words elsewhere. There is one parallel: Warner's Menechmus, harried by the doctor, speaks of 'birdes that beare feathers, or fishes that have finnes' (Bullough, I, 33); in a very different context both Dromios, one inside and one outside Antipholus of Ephesus's door, speak of fowls that have no feathers and fish that have no fin (3.1.79, 82). This tells us nothing about influences, for the phrases sound very like separate memories of a proverb. That both writers turn Plautus's bracelet (*spinter*) into a chain is also of no consequence, as it is sometimes said to be; it could be a coincidence, or, if an echo, one that could have worked in either direction – in any case, Shakespeare turned the *spinter* into a necklace-chain, while Warner gave a chain of no specific kind.

No direct connection between Warner and Shakespeare has been established. We come back to the language in which Shakespeare read Plautus. He must have read the *Amphitruo*, the *Rudens* (see p. 10 below), and the *Mostellaria* in Latin (it is unlikely that he went to Continental versions), for there appear to have been no English translations of these plays earlier than the date of *The Comedy of Errors*; if he could do that, as of course he could, he could also read the *Menaechmi* in Latin, and we need not doubt that he did so.

Another comedy of awkward encounters is George Gascoigne's *Supposes*.[1] This play, a free translation of Ariosto's *I Suppositi* ('The Masqueraders' or 'The Substitutes'), was acted at Gray's Inn in 1566, later at Oxford and at Trinity College, Cambridge, and published in 1575. The errors, or 'supposes', come about because, in Gascoigne's words, we see 'the master supposed for the servant, the servant for the master: the freeman for a slave, and the bondslave for a freeman: the stranger for a well known friend, and the familiar for a stranger'; also because, of her three suitors, Polynesta loves only Dulippo, a feigned servant of the household. *Supposes* has, probably with justice, been regarded as an analogue of *Errors*. Among other playwrights, John Lyly is a writer to whom Shakespeare owed much – more than some of the verse-style in his early plays. His *Mother Bombie* is a jumble of errors and embarrassments, at some points not unlike *Errors* in spirit.[2] Four old men, their servants (one of them named Dromio), three young men, and three young women are involved in a series of entanglements in which some characters assume identities that are not their own, and love-stratagems are managed chiefly by the servants (these and the old men recall Terence's witty slaves and old men). Foakes has noted[3] half a dozen verbal parallels with Shakespeare's play, but some of these are commonplaces of the period. The debt to Lyly is 'general and pervasive' rather than specific, seen most clearly in the style and in the spirit of the comic exchanges and

---

[1] *Supposes* is a source for *The Taming of the Shrew* (Bullough, *Sources*, I, 111–58).
[2] Hazlitt, somewhat unkindly, says of this play that 'it is what its name would import, old, quaint, and vulgar. . . It is little else than a tissue of absurd mistakes, arising from the confusion of the different characters one with another, like another Comedy of Errors, and ends in their being (most of them), married in a game at cross-purposes to the persons they particularly dislike.' (*The Complete Works of William Hazlitt*, ed. P. P. Howe, 21 vols., 1930, 6, pp. 197–8.) Hazlitt thought little better of *The Comedy of Errors* (*Works*, 4, pp. 351–3).   [3] Foakes, p. xxxiii.

the relations between masters and servants. No more than *Supposes* is *Mother Bombie* a source for *The Comedy of Errors*, but both may have played some part in its background.

The tale of Apollonius of Tyre narrated by Gower in Book VIII of *Confessio Amantis* seems to be the main source for the romantic side of the play, Egeon's adventures and his discovery of his long-lost wife.[1] Apollonius's wife Lucina, on board a ship, gives birth to a daughter, and then appears to die. Her body is thrown overboard in a coffer, which floats to Ephesus. She finds her way to the temple of Diana, where she becomes one of the sisterhood. Some years later Apollonius is told in a vision to go to the temple at Ephesus, and does so; having made his shrift, he recounts his adventures 'in open Audience'. Lucina, now the abbess, hears him, and the two are joyfully reunited. The parallels are clear. Gower's tale contributes nothing beyond Egeon's history, which of course is important, but it may have been his influence, combined with that of the Bible, that led Shakespeare to choose Ephesus as the scene of his action.

Similar events occur in a number of romances. In Sidney's *Arcadia*, for example, the friends Musidorus and Pyrocles suffer shipwreck. Musidorus is brought ashore clinging to a 'square small coffer'. Pyrocles takes hold of a floating mast, and after a fight with pirates has taken place, is picked up by a passing ship. The two are later reunited.[2] *Arcadia* is at least an analogue of *The Comedy of Errors*.

For other elements in the story of loss and recovery Shakespeare may have taken hints from another work by Plautus, the *Rudens*, one of the more 'romantic' of his plays. Here again, as in Egeon's story, there is a child (this time a girl, Palaestra), who is stolen from her father, an elderly Athenian living on the coast of Cyrene near a temple of Venus; grown up, she is taken by a procurer aboard a ship bound for Sicily, is shipwrecked, but manages to return to land, where she is succoured by the priestess of the temple. I am not suggesting that this is directly a source for *The Comedy of Errors*; it is perhaps rather an analogue. It is, however, much more closely an analogue of *Pericles*.

The Bible, always present to Shakespeare, did two things in particular for him, I think, when he was writing this play: it helped him to refine the atmosphere that he wanted to evoke in his Ephesus – he avoided the coarse and immoral aspects of Plautus's Epidamnus; and it encouraged him to impart moral feeling to his comedy – an important addition to what he found in his sources.[3] In the Acts of the Apostles he would have read that Paul 'passed thorow the upper coasts, and came to Ephesus . . . so all they which dwelt in Asia, hearde the worde of the Lorde Jesus' (Acts 19.1, 10). There too he would have read that 'certaine of the vagabond Jewes, exorcistes, tooke upon them to call ouer them which had evill spirits, the name of the Lord Jesus' (v. 13), and that many 'which used curious craftes, brought their bookes, and burned them' (v. 19). This would be enough to suggest the addition of jugglers, sorcerers and witches to the swindlers and

---

[1] Gower's narrative is a source for *Pericles*.

[2] Sir Philip Sidney, *The Countess of Pembroke's Arcadia*, ed. Maurice Evans, 1977, pp. 64–8.

[3] Noble (pp. 58–76) shows that Shakespeare knew well at least two English translations of the Bible – the Geneva version of 1560 (perhaps in a later revision), and the Bishops' Bible, published in 1568 and reprinted with minor variants in accidentals in 1591. He seems to have used the Bishops' Bible in his early plays, and both translations from about the middle 1590s. Since we know that he kept his reading up to date, it is probable that he used the 1591 Bishops' Bible for *Errors*, and it is from this that my quotations are taken. We may have here a further clue to the dating.

ol.3.11.   22 *Wiues, submit your selus vnto your owne husbands, as vnto the Lord:

Cor.11.3   23 *For the husbande is the head of the wife, euen as Christ is ye head of the Church, and he is the sauiour of the body.

24 But as the Church is subiect vnto Christ, likewise the wiues to their owne husbands in all things.

Co.3.19.   25 *Ye husbandes loue your wiues, euen as Christ also loued the Church, and gaue himselfe for it,

26 To sanctifie it, when hee had cleansed it in the b fountaine of water in the word:

b Baptisme is
a tot that
Baptisme con-
secrateth the
thing to him
selfe, make it
holp his
worthat is,
his prise of
free ifica-
tion it yit.

27 That he might present it vnto himselfe a glorious Church, not hauing spot or wrinkle, or any such thing; but that it should bee holy, and without blame.

28 So ought men to loue their wiues, as their owne bodies: hee that loueth his wife, loueth himselfe.

1 Ephesians 5.22–8 from the 1591 edition of the Bishops' Bible

con-men he found in Plautus and used in Antipholus's catalogue at the end of the play's second scene. Later verses of the same chapter gave him the priory (also in Gower) in which the Abbess reigned supreme, for Paul spoke of 'the temple of the great goddesse Diana' and the cry of her worshippers, 'Great is Diana of the Ephesians.'

St Paul's Epistle to the Ephesians supplied material of a moral nature, especially in its fourth, fifth, and sixth chapters. From the fifth came the teachings with which Luciana and the Abbess respond to Adriana's complaints about her husband's apparent misbehaviour and indifference to her. St Paul's admonition beginning, 'Wiues, submit your selues vnto your owne husbands, as vnto the Lord', is directly echoed by Luciana (at 2.1.6–24, for example), and less directly by the Abbess (5.1.68–86): 'A man is master of his liberty'; all creatures 'Are their males' subjects, and at their controls'; men 'Are masters to their females, and their lords'; in all his pursuits 'To be disturbed, would mad or man or beast.' Similarly, when masters and servants are at variance with one another, Shakespeare draws on Ephesians 6.5–17: 'Seruants, obey them that are your bodily masters . . . And ye masters, do the same things vnto them, putting away threatnings.' In the play the effect of these Pauline admonitions is complicated by the comedy of misapprehension – Adriana has two identical husbands, and exasperated masters beat their uncomprehending faithful servants. The play is rich in biblical echoes; others are referred to in the commentary.

Bullough reproduces (vol. 1) Warner's version of the *Menaechmi*, much of E. H. Sugden's translation of the *Amphitruo* (1893), and passages from Gower as sources for *Errors*, and *Supposes* as a source for *The Shrew*. Warner may also be read in parallel with the Latin in W. H. D. Rouse's volume in the Shakespeare Classics, *The Menaechmi: The Original of Shakespeare's Comedy of Errors*. All of Plautus's extant plays, with translations by Paul Dixon, are to be found in the parallel-text series of the Loeb Classical Library. Relevant passages from the New Testament are provided in Appendix 2, pp. 113–14 below.

The play

The Comedy of Errors is not only very good theatre, it is also very good reading. It is a finely-balanced mixture of pathos and suspense, illusion and delusion, love turned bitter and love that is sweet, farce and fun. The fun begins in the second scene with the entry of the Syracusan pair and is sustained with great verve and vivacity through the next three acts. It arises from the farce of mistaken identity which is the stuff and substance of the play – from all the improbabilities that result from the use of two pairs of identical twins who in the course of a single day repeatedly encounter people whom they *know* they know, but do not know. 'If we are in for improbability', said Dowden,[1] 'let us at least be repaid for it by fun, and have that in abundance. Let the incredibility become a twofold incredibility, and it is none the worse.' The fun is of course greatly increased by our knowledge of everything that the characters in the play do not know. Even if Shakespeare did not at all times make clear in the dialogue who is who, we should know from his looks and voice who is speaking to whom. One would suppose that no producer in his senses would put on the stage two pairs of actors who could not be told apart. The only possible surprise for us is the advent of the Abbess in the final episodes, and that should not be much of a surprise, for we have learnt from romances that if a wife disappears at the beginning she is more likely than not to reappear at the end.

The keynotes of the play are illusion and delusion. The Abbess and Egeon are the only persons who are not wholly deluded by appearances, and even they are so far deceived as not to know that all their family are alive and well, and close at hand in Ephesus; and Egeon is, naturally enough, bewildered when he is unexpectedly faced by two sons who cannot be told from each other even by a wife and two personal slaves. The illusion, like the fun, begins in the second scene when the visiting Antipholus is accosted by a slave whom he *knows* to be his own Dromio, who precipitately tells him that his dinner is spoiling and he must hurry home, and who emphatically denies that he has in his keeping money that Antipholus has entrusted to him. Newly arrived in Ephesus, he has been thinking about his long and seemingly hopeless quest, and has felt that he is

> like a drop of water
> That in the ocean seeks another drop,
> Who, falling there to find his fellow forth,
> Unseen, inquisitive, confounds himself.   (1.2.35–8)

After his encounter with the wrong Dromio he recalls having been told that Ephesus

---

[1] Dowden, p. 57.

2   Komisarjevsky's production, Stratford-upon-Avon, 1938: Dennis Roberts as Dromio of Syracuse (at window), C. Rivers Gadsby as Pinch (centre, hatless), G. Kay Souper as Balthasar (in braces), Donald L. Smith as the Duke's attendant (top hat with feather)

> is full of cozenage,
> As nimble jugglers that deceive the eye,
> Dark-working sorcerers that change the mind,
> Soul-killing witches that deform the body,
> Disguisèd cheaters, prating mountebanks,
> And many suchlike liberties of sin.   (1.2.97–102)

The Roman-style comedy of misunderstanding is teasingly haunted by moral implications owed to the distant echoes of St Paul. The phrase 'liberties of sin' could not have come from Plautus, and suggests that those who fall under the spells of Ephesus are in need of spiritual conversion as well as material enlightenment. The mind of Antipholus of Syracuse remains 'changed' until the end of the play. A little later in the day, when Adriana claims him as her husband, he is led to wonder whether he was married to her in a dream from which he is not yet awake (2.2.173–4). His Dromio, too, is struck with a horrified wonder:

> This is the fairy land. O spite of spites,
> We talk with goblins, owls, and sprites.   (2.2.180–1)

So it continues. He wonders whether he is 'in earth, in heaven, or in hell'. When Dromio brings him money to save him from the imprisonment with which his brother is threatened, he *knows* that he is wandering 'in illusions' (4.3.36), and when, immediately after this, he is greeted as an old friend by the Courtesan, he *knows* that she is the devil (43), and Dromio agrees that she is at least 'the devil's dam'.

All the other figures in the farce are similarly bemused by error. The Duke thinks that they 'all have drunk of Circe's cup'. Antipholus of Ephesus in all his encounters thinks the wrong to be the right person. His wife more than once believes the other Antipholus to be her husband (as does Luciana), not only when she is entertaining him in her home, but even at the very end. 'Which of you two did dine with me today?' she asks (5.1.369). Luciana is surprised, and not a little shocked, when she is so warmly and elegantly courted by her brother-in-law, as she supposes Antipholus of Syracuse to be; perhaps, nevertheless, she enjoys a little quiet fun in hearing him, and in reporting him to her sister – nothing in this play is to be taken too seriously. Strangely, we are not told at the end that she is to be a wife – she and Antipholus would make a gentle and happy pair. In the theatre the swiftness of the action allows us no time to wonder at all these mistaken beliefs and weird occurrences; everywhere, as Johnson says, '*Shakespeare* approximates the remote, and familiarizes the wonderful.'

Most of Shakespeare's comedies contain pathos, separations within families, or potential tragedy. *The Comedy of Errors* is no exception. In strong contrast to Plautus's jaunty prologue, Shakespeare opens with the pathetic figure of Egeon, standing in peril of his life. Although at the back of our minds we know from the title and from our reading of romances that in the end all will be well, we must, while he is before us, feel deeply for Egeon as he tells his woeful story, and is told that, unless someone can within the day find a thousand marks to redeem him, he must die – just as we feel deeply for the later heroines who must suffer deprivation or banishment or cruelty before they are brought to happiness – Rosalind or Viola or Hermione. The pathos returns briefly in the final scene, together with a touch of suspense, when Egeon is led in with the Headsman, and again when he is bewildered by the sudden appearance of his long-lost wife and son. These moments are in keeping with all the earlier improbabilities, but they are not farcical. That they follow so hard upon the binding of the one Antipholus and the narrow escape of the other from being locked up as a madman makes the final reunion all the happier. That the close of the play should be placed in the hands of the slaves is a final incidence of fun, and, in this particular play, entirely appropriate.

It is commonly said that in farce situation is everything, characterisation little or nothing. Shakespeare knew better. In Johnson's phrase, he drew his characters, like his scenes, 'from nature and from life'. To every one of his characters he gave an individuality of his own and a distinctive voice; it is a skill that enlarges farce into comedy.

The Dromios are not, as is often said, as like as two peas. Dromio of Ephesus is the more sprightly, and the more in command of all the tricks of language that make for the comic and the witty. His opening lines are the first irruption in the play of high comedy, not only for their shock-effect on the recently-arrived Antipholus, but also in their masterly display of the rhetorical device called *anadiplosis*, by which words at the end of one line are picked up at the beginning of the next. As an introduction to Dromio, to his idiom, to the treatment that a slave expects to receive, and to the spirit of the play, the whole speech is worth quoting:

Returned so soon? Rather approached too late.
The capon burns, the pig falls from the spit.
The clock hath strucken twelve upon the bell;
My mistress made it one upon my cheek.
She is so hot because the meat is cold.
The meat is cold because you come not home.
You come not home because you have no stomach.
You have no stomach, having broke your fast.
But we that know what 'tis to fast and pray
Are penitent for your default today.   (1.2.43–52)

This playing upon words is characteristic of his voice, and, like all witty slaves, he has at
his disposal a fund of proverbial wisdom. His Syracusan twin is less voluble, less
ebullient; his comedy (apart from his drubbings) is more dependent on puns and
proverbs. However, he shows some spirit when he is barring the entry of the Ephesians
into their own house, and when he is describing Nell (3.2.77–130).

Nor are the Antipholuses, except in their appearance, alike. Weary with travel and
sorrow, Antipholus of Syracuse is quiet and despondent, though quick enough, at the
contrariness of slaves, to flare into anger and strike blows. When not harassed, he is
gentle and courtly, given to calling ladies 'fair dame' or 'gentle mistress', and he is
eloquent in his wooing – we must hope Luciana in the end said yes. The other
Antipholus is more robust, ready to smash down a door (though his own) if it keeps him
from his dinner. He feels a little henpecked, and is ready to seek comfort from a woman
who is not his wife and to ask his goldsmith to make his excuses for him. He is embroiled
in the same kinds of confusions as his twin, but reacts to them by beating slaves and not
by sinking into dismay and despair; he is, or thinks he is, secure in his knowledge of
Ephesus, and his knowledge that he knows everyone who needs to be known. He has for
many years been held in high favour by the Duke, and is, in the opinion of his fellow
citizens,

Of very reverend reputation, . . .
Of credit infinite, highly beloved,
Second to none that lives here in the city.   (5.1.5–7)

He is a man of substance. He lives in a large house of two storeys ('Husband, I'll dine
above with you today', says Adriana), probably with a balcony (see pp. 23–4 below), and
has, for Shakespeare's purposes in 3.1, six maidservants in addition to his slave and a
kitchen-maid.

The women of the play stand out more vividly than the men. The two who might have
been twins – how thankful we are that they are only sisters – are more clearly
differentiated than the pairs who really are twins. Adriana is temperamental; she nags
her husband to the last, even complaining of him to the Abbess, but wails at great length
when in exasperation he sometimes goes off to find congenial company elsewhere – after
all, she keeps a good house and is herself faithful. She needs to be taught a lesson or two
by her more even-tempered sister. In her worse moments she thinks Antipholus to be

> deformèd, crooked, old, and sere;
> Ill-faced, worse-bodied, shapeless everywhere;
> Vicious, ungentle, foolish, blunt, unkind,
> Stigmatical in making, worse in mind. (4.2.19–22)

When she thinks he is going to be put in jail or a madhouse, she rushes to his help and calls him 'gentle husband'. Naughty as he is, she loves him dearly, as indeed she has from the beginning, if too possessively; even her sharpest railings have come from her mouth, not her heart, as she has shown in her dialogue with Luciana at the end of 2.1, and, in so many words, in 4.2.18, 28. She will, we trust, when she has been shown her own faults, behave better in the future.

Luciana is somewhat given to preaching (as is the Abbess, but then that is her vocation) and at the same time a very agreeable and pleasantly-spoken young woman, as she was when played by Francesca Annis, with Judi Dench beside her as a not too querulous Adriana. She is of course disconcerted when Antipholus woos her so fervently,[1] thinks that perhaps he is mad, but after her first sermon does little to stop him, and can scarcely be said to chide him as she chides Adriana. She is as anxious about her brother-in-law's welfare as her sister, and would be incapable of reviling him, as Adriana does. The gentle Antipholus knows what he is saying when he addresses her as 'Sweet mistress'.

From Dromio's graphic portrait we know all we want to know about Nell – globose, sweaty, red nose, bad of breath. Out of Plautus's courtesan Erotium Shakespeare fashioned someone entirely new. Erotium is exactly what the word courtesan means, what would at one time have been called a gold-digger, ready to clutch at cloaks or bracelets or 'brass'. Shakespeare's unnamed Courtesan is different. Of course she likes being given presents (who doesn't?) and would not have her own costly jewellery go astray, but she can scarcely be said to be rapacious, even if she is as much concerned for her lost baubles as for what appears to be Antipholus's madness. She is good company, 'of excellent discourse, Pretty and witty; wild, and yet, too, gentle' (gentle in both the modern sense and in the usual Elizabethan sense of 'well-bred', though Antipholus of Syracuse thinks otherwise) – just the kind of girl a sensible man would look for if he had a nagging wife. Her wildness is not seen, and there is no vice in her. Shakespeare chose to celebrate the loves and marriages of nice young women rather than fornication.

All the lesser figures contribute something. Doctor Pinch, Plautus's *medicus* new-apparelled, can be quickly disposed of; it is enough to quote Antipholus of Ephesus:

> one Pinch, a hungry, lean-faced villain,
> A mere anatomy, a mountebank,
> A threadbare juggler and a fortune-teller,
> A needy, hollow-eyed, sharp-looking wretch,
> A living dead man – (5.1.238–42)

a magnificently Shakespearean vignette. We may note in passing that, although in his introductory stage direction he is called a Schoolmaster, in the dialogue he is

---

[1] Johnson did not approve of Antipholus's way of addressing Luciana: 'When he calls the girl his *only heaven on the earth*, he utters the common cant of lovers. When he calls her *his heaven's claim*, I cannot understand him.'

3   Clifford Williams's production, Stratford-upon-Avon, 1962: Susan Maryott as Luciana and Alec McCowen as Antipholus of Syracuse

always addressed, referred to, and in his pretentious way behaves, as a conjurer.

Another moment of exquisite comedy is provided by the officious and boldly-spoken Jailer; he has had the Ephesian pair carried off to prison, and is rounding off the case, when he is suddenly confronted by Antipholus of Syracuse (yet once more taken for his twin) and Dromio, with rapiers in their hands. Let the situation speak for itself:

> LUCIANA God, for thy mercy, they are loose again!
> ADRIANA And come with naked swords. Let's call more help
>   To have them bound again.
> JAILER   Away, they'll kill us!
> *Exeunt omnes [apart from Antipholus S. and Dromio S.], as fast as may be, frighted* (4.4.138–40)

The devil–witch–courtesan, now apparently at one with Adriana, is one of those that run away as fast as may be. For the first time Antipholus and Dromio feel they have the upper hand of the terrifying creatures that beset them. 'I see these witches are afraid of swords', Antipholus drily comments, and at last Dromio 'could find it in [his] heart to stay [in Ephesus] still, and turn witch'. He is disposed to join what St Paul called 'the users of curious crafts'.

There remains a very important character, the Abbess. She, 'a virtuous and a reverend lady', is a splendid figure, a woman of great authority and, we must feel, of commanding presence; for the most part of few words, and those always to the point and peremptory.

'Be quiet, people', she says as she comes in upon a brabble, and tumult turns to mere clamour; a little later, firmly, 'Whoever bound him, I will loose his bonds.' She will not kow-tow to the Duke, as the sisters do; her power is as great as his. She will have no nonsense, has no patience with nagging wives and tells them so; Adriana has to put up with a severe scolding from her. It does not take this competent and formidable woman long to straighten out all the entanglements of the day; chaos gives way to order, confusion of mind to practical good sense. The Bible has taught her, as it has (at times) taught Luciana, to see clearly. Shakespeare wittily conjoins the idea he found in Acts 19.26, that the whole city of Ephesus was 'full of confusion', with the *epitasis*, or thickening of the plot, in Roman comedy. The Abbess offers proper Pauline counsel to those who come to hear her, and she is the *dea ex machina* who resolves the play's complications in its *catastrophe*. It is she who, in her final words, 'After so long grief, such nativity', sums up the theme of regeneration with which the play is brought to its conclusion. We rejoice with her when, after the long years, her husband and her sons are restored to her, and we wish that we could celebrate with her at her well-organised 'gossips' feast'.

Presentation

'To the unities of time and place he has shewn no regard', said Johnson. This is not quite true. In *The Comedy of Errors* and *The Tempest* Shakespeare shows regard to both these unities; the events take place within a single day, in the one play in a market-place, in the other on a remote island. This compression much increases the force, in *The Comedy of Errors*, of the torrent of confusions. For the unity of action he has none of the reverence of Renaissance scholars – his overflowing mind would have found it far too restrictive; in both plays there are plots within plots.

His use of language already shows all the versatility, if not quite the maturity, that he shows a few years later. He moves easily between verse and prose, between blank and rhymed verse, between verse that is grave and verse that is pretty or witty. When they are explaining or complaining or receiving or evading blows his slaves use prose, but Dromio of Ephesus can burst into splendidly ebullient poetry. I have quoted lines in which Shakespeare allows him a very striking use of *anadiplosis*. Not quite the same, but in their effectiveness very similar, are some later lines in which he again makes a telling use of his rhythms and his repetitions:

> When I desired him to come home to dinner
> He asked me for a thousand marks in gold.
> ''Tis dinner-time', quoth I. 'My gold', quoth he.
> 'Your meat doth burn', quoth I. 'My gold', quoth he.
> 'Will you come home?' quoth I. 'My gold', quoth he.
> 'Where is the thousand marks I gave thee, villain?'
> 'The pig', quoth I, 'is burned.' 'My gold', quoth he.
> 'My mistress, sir –' quoth I. 'Hang up thy mistress!
> I know not thy mistress. Out on thy mistress!'   (2.1.58–66)

In a play in which action is so very important, especially in entrances and exits, it is startling to come across a passage of decorative and evocative writing. After Egeon and the Duke, the twins falling over one another, Adriana's complaints, and Luciana's somewhat sententious wisdom, Antipholus's wooing of Luciana sounds a strain not heard elsewhere in the play:

> O, train me not, sweet mermaid, with thy note
>   To drown me in thy sister's flood of tears.
> Sing, siren, for thyself, and I will dote.
>   Spread o'er the silver waves thy golden hairs
> And as a bed I'll take thee, and there lie,
>   And in that glorious supposition think
> He gains by death that hath such means to die.   (3.2.45–51)

In a very different vein the Abbess's rebuke to Adriana (5.1.68–86) is very powerful in its imagery of the poison and disease and other foes to life that will follow 'the venom clamours of a jealous woman'. In this play strong feelings, whether of love or of outrage or of sorrow, bring out of Shakespeare's characters the most memorable poetry. Another speech which comes to mind again and again is Egeon's bewildered lament when his son does not know him:

> Not know my voice? O time's extremity,
> Hast thou so cracked and splitted my poor tongue
> In seven short years that here my only son
> Knows not my feeble key of untuned cares?
> Though now this grainèd face of mine be hid
> In sap-consuming winter's drizzled snow,
> And all the conduits of my blood froze up,
> Yet hath my night of life some memory,
> My wasting lamps some fading glimmer left,
> My dull deaf ears a little use to hear.   (5.1.307–16)

Here the effect is gained of course from the situation, but even more from the closely packed imagery expressive of failing faculties and desolation.

Money and gold are an important theme of the play and sustain much of its imagery and word-play (such as that on 'marks'). Food too is prominent, and there are some transiently recurring images, like that of the water-drop lost in the ocean (1.2.35–6, 2.2.117), but there are no obvious chains of recurrent imagery running all the way through the play such as Caroline Spurgeon found in most of Shakespeare's plays.[1] The nearest to this can be seen in the legal terminology. There are about a dozen legal terms in the first scene, more than are strictly necessary to tell an old man, 'his goods confiscate to the Duke's dispose', that he is suffering because he has 'infringed our laws' in Ephesus, and that he must 'quit the penalty', as has been 'decreed' 'in solemn synods'. Other merchants 'have sealed [these] rigorous statutes with their bloods' (word-play here), 'Therefore by law thou art condemned to die.' These references, continuing in the same scene, are picked up in the next by the Merchant, and again later (2.2.69–71) in some word-play on 'fine and recovery'; there are some puns on 'band' and 'bond', and the language of the law is of course used when towards the end the action turns on seizure, arrest, and imprisonment. This could hardly be accidental, especially when the strongest impact is made in the opening scene of the play. If, as is not improbable, *The*

[1] Caroline F. E. Spurgeon, *Shakespeare's Imagery and What It Tells Us*, 1935.

Comedy of Errors was written to be performed for the first time before a legal audience, the young men of, let us say, one of the Inns of Court would have enjoyed the use in a play of their own jargon, as they would have enjoyed, in the verbal sparring between masters and servants, an echo of their own witty disputations.

The play has often invited musical adaptation, but in the changing poise and pace of its verbal art it has a music of its own. For sober or grave passages the medium is habitually blank verse: the Duke and Egeon, the Abbess, the masters when they are not upbraiding or jesting with the slaves, Adriana (often) in her plaintive moods, the courtesan when she is worried, the merchants, and Angelo. However, there is much rhymed verse, whether in couplets or in 'stanzas', especially in lines given to Luciana and Adriana. There are in 3.1 and elsewhere some rhyming hexameters, at times regular, at times a little slipshod, and occasionally, as is not out of place in a rollicking comedy, there is downright doggerel, especially from the slaves. Shakespeare's virtuosity is best exemplified in the scene which begins with Antipholus's attempt to win the heart of Luciana. The variations in the movement, from Luciana's reproaches to Antipholus's lyrical wooing, on to Dromio's lively description of greasy Nell and then to Antipholus's anxiety and perplexity; the modulation from quatrains (interspersed with hypermetric rhymes) to couplets in stichomythia, to couplets sustained, to prose, and finally to blank verse: these transitions, though lacking the precision and balance of the recurrent themes, are the speaking and theatrical equivalents of the concertos of such baroque composers as Vivaldi or Pergolesi or Salieri. And while it may lack the exquisite melodies, the interchanges of fun and fantasy in the play invite comparison with some such opera as *The Magic Flute*. (In a Theatre Set-up performance in the nave of Fountains Abbey, in the summer of 1986, the closing moments were delightfully, and fittingly, accompanied by the music of the Papageno–Papagena duet.)

Staging

We do not know of any performance of *The Comedy of Errors* earlier than that which took place at Gray's Inn on the night of Innocents' Day, 28 December 1594. A description of the occasion on which it was performed has come down to us in the *Gesta Grayorum*,[1] an account of the revels which were enjoyed at the Inn during the Christmas season of 1594–5. We know also that the play was staged at Court ten years later. The source of our knowledge is the Revels Accounts, a record of plays and masques kept at the Revels Office and submitted to the Treasurer of the Chamber for the payment of the players. In the record of the Christmas festivities at Court in 1604 we are told that 'On Inosents night The plaie of Errors', by 'Shaxberd', was performed 'By his Maiesties plaiers'.[2]

We cannot know today just how *Errors* was staged on these two occasions, but at least for the performance at Gray's Inn we have, from our reading of the *Gesta*, reasonable grounds for conjecture. Three hypotheses seem tenable: one put forward by Chambers and Greg[3] and followed by some later scholars; a second envisaged by myself when I revisited the Inn; a third suggested to me by Mr Walter Hodges.

---

[1] *Gesta Grayorum: or, The History of the High and Mighty Prince Henry, Prince of Purpoole . . . Who Reigned and Died, A.D. 1594*, printed 1688, reproduced in a Malone Society reprint, ed. W. W. Greg, 1914. See Appendix 1, pp. 111–12 below.

[2] Chambers, *WS*, II, 331.   [3] Chambers, *WS*, I, 307–8; Greg, *SF*, p. 200.

4   A stage set from *Terentius 'Comediae'* (1493)

In 1493, about a hundred years before Shakespeare wrote the play, Johann Trechsel published at Lyons an edition of Terence's plays containing the first known illustrations of early Renaissance stage sets for Roman comedies. I reproduce one of these (illustration 4), showing a scene in *Andria*. At the back of the stage are four adjacent 'houses' from which the actors emerge through curtains to play their parts; above the houses are panels indicating, by names and symbols, their ownership and (probably) the callings of the owners. This was obviously one way in which Roman plays were staged in Trechsel's time; it may also have been one of the ways in which 'Latin' plays were staged in Elizabethan times. Also reproduced (illustration 5) is a 'comic stage' pictured in the mid sixteenth century by Sebastiano Serlio, showing houses in a street scene, and again symbols, such as a cardinal's hat and a scorpion above a Gothic window.

As at the other Inns of Court, the Christmas Revels at Gray's Inn ran from the eve of the Feast of St Thomas (20 December) until Shrovetide (the day before Ash Wednesday). The Inns elected a member to preside as Lord of Misrule. At Gray's Inn he was called the Prince of Purpoole – a corruption, according to Quiller-Couch,[1] 'facetiously borrowed from Porte Poule Lane, by Gray's Inn' (Portpool Lane still runs into Gray's Inn Road opposite the north end of the Inn); according to Margaret Knapp and Michael Kobialka,[2] it was taken from Portpool, the parish (they ought more properly to have said

---

[1] NS, p. vii.

[2] Margaret Knapp and Michael Kobialka, 'The Prince of Purpoole: the 1594 production of *The Comedy of Errors* at Gray's Inn Hall', *Theatre History Studies* 4 (1984), 71–81.

Scena Comica.

5 A mid-sixteenth-century *scena comica* by Sebastiano Serlio

the Manor) in which the Inn was situated. For the 1594 Revels the Prince of Purpoole was Henry Helmes of Norfolk.

Such a stage set as Trechsel's, if not Serlio's, could have been provided in the hall of Gray's Inn for the playing of *Errors*. Built between 1556 and 1569, the hall has retained, in spite of some renovation in 1826, a very fine Tudor interior, 70 feet long, almost 35 feet wide, 47 feet high. At the top end was a dais, nine or ten feet deep, carrying the high table. Before it was the 'Ancients' Table' at which senior members of the Inn for whom there was not room on the high table took their meals; further forward a fireplace, which no longer remains. The students' tables stood parallel to the walls.[1] The hall was partially destroyed during the second world war, but the fine west end suffered comparatively little damage, and the whole has been beautifully restored.

For the first reconstruction we must visualise a stage – the mart of Ephesus – backed by three houses, perhaps adjoining one another, perhaps, as Chambers and Greg thought, separated by streets, one of them leading to the port.[2] In such a set as this I would prefer to see the houses side by side, the road to the port being by way of a side-exit. The house-fronts would presumably be some three feet from the back of the hall (perhaps two would be enough, to give more front stage), so that the actors could pass from one side to the other as required by the action.

In the centre the priory, the most important building, is marked with a cross or some

[1] Sir Dunbar Plunket Barton, *Gray's Inn*, 1937; Knapp and Kobialka, 'Prince of Purpoole', p. 74.
[2] See Chambers, *WS*, I, 307–8.

6   The Elizabethan screen at the west end of the Great Hall of Gray's Inn

other religious emblem. On the one side is the house of the substantial and highly-regarded Antipholus, bearing the sign of a Phoenix. In this version of the stage it has a balcony[1] on which (in 3.1) Luce and Adriana, when they *Enter* briefly, may be seen (*above*) by the audience while being invisible to the clamouring group below. On the other side of the priory is the Courtesan's house, with the sign of a Porcupine. The doors of the houses are made of wood (they are not curtains); one of them is banged hard, and needs an 'iron crow' if it is to be broken down.

Such a reconstruction as this seems to take for granted that the stage required for the performance was set up over the dais at the east end of the hall, and that the 'houses', including one with a balcony, were built for the occasion at the back of this stage. The account of the evening that has come down to us makes this seem very unlikely (see Appendix 1, pp. 111–12, below). A second visit to the hall has persuaded me that the building of such a set would have been wasted labour, and that a very suitable, I would say ideal, alternative lay ready to hand.

A richly carved oak screen, reputedly the gift of Queen Elizabeth, extends across the whole breadth of the hall at its west end. It holds five handsome arched doorways with finely carved doors. Above the screen there is a gallery fronted by a solid balustrade supported by male and female busts standing on corbels. All this is clearly seen in illustration 6 and in the frontispiece, which is a photograph taken from the dais at the

---

[1] See Greg, *SF*, p. 200.

eastern end. Most fortunately the screen stands in the part of the hall that suffered least from the wartime bombing.

It seems to me very probable that the stage that we are told was built for the Innocents' Day festivities of 1594 was set up at the western end of the hall along the screen. It is possible – indeed likely – that a stage was assembled for other 'grand Nights' during Revels at the Inn; such a structure as I visualise would have been suitable for many kinds of plays (and other entertainments); the opening of one of the doors in the screen would have provided an inner stage, if it was required, and the gallery an upper stage. The stage, extending across the breadth of the hall, could be easily and rapidly assembled in sections, which would be kept in store for use on other such occasions. The central section would not have been set in place until the Prince, accompanied on this particular evening by distinguished visitors from the Inner Temple, had made his ceremonial entry through the central door, to be formally greeted by student 'officers' (possibly even by Master Benchers), and, when it was appropriate, to proceed to his throne on the stage.

I suggest that for *The Comedy of Errors*, as it was acted in the hall, the three inner doors, appropriately marked as in the previous reconstruction, would have served admirably as the entrances to the houses of Antipholus and the Courtesan, and to the priory. The two outer doors could well have been left open to represent the ways leading to the port and the city; they could indeed have served for any entrances and exits for which stage directions do not specify particular points of entry or departure. The gallery would, in 3.1, allow Luce and Adriana to appear (*above*) to the view of the audience, while remaining, as they stood back a little, hidden by the balustrade from the group below. I am not sure how Dromio of Syracuse would have been represented (*within*). Perhaps, in a hall, he could have been heard through a chink in the door as he shouted his abuse (with one exception his speeches are single lines); more probably he would have made himself visible to the audience by standing just within the open outer door adjacent to that of Antipholus's house.

Something similar to the stage sets that have been postulated here could have been provided at Court for the Christmas festivities of 1604 (or in other great halls); many of the courtiers had been Gray's Inn men, and some of them might have recalled the performance of 1594. I cannot suggest just how the play might have been staged if it had been performed in a public theatre. However, in *The First Night of 'Twelfth Night'*, 1954, pp. 69–77, Leslie Hotson argues that 'small structural units of frame and canvas called *mansions* or *houses*, . . . with practicable doors, or with curtains', must frequently have been used on the public stages (as also at Court on a stage placed in the centre of the hall). If *Errors* was ever publicly played, it is possible that three such *houses* were set on the stage for its performance.

Obviously cost was not spared in the Gray's Inn Revels; a manuscript of 1586 (among the Burghley Papers) tells us that this Inn was the most prosperous of the legal foundations.[1] As well as the 'very good Inventions and Conceipts' mentioned in the *Gesta Grayorum* account of this particular night, the Ambassador from the 'Emperor' of the Inner Temple, '*Frederick Templarius*', and his entourage were 'very gallantly

[1] Knapp and Kobialka, 'Prince of Purpoole', p. 73.

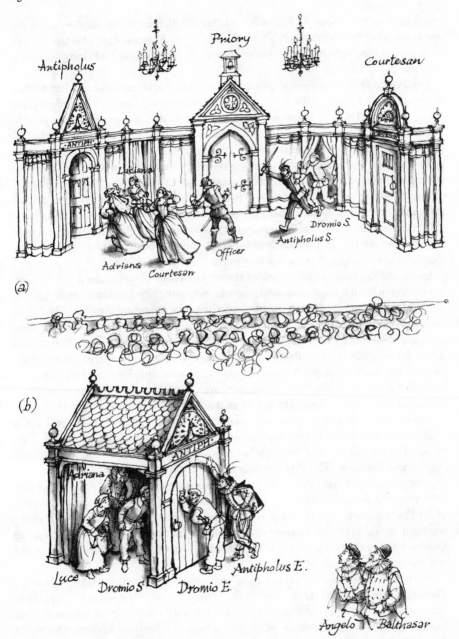

7 Imagined settings for performances, with 'houses' in the late-medieval manner, by C. Walter Hodges
a Act 4, Scene 4, set on a hall stage, the 'houses' represented by doors similar to those shown in illustration 4
b Act 3, Scene 1: a self-standing 'house' arranged as one of several for acting in the middle of the hall with or without a stage

appointed', as the Prince of Purpoole and 'his Gentlemen-Pensioners' were on the previous night, 'the first grand Night' of the festivities. A special stage was built for the occasion – according to the first reconstruction at the east end of the hall, in my version at the west.

The Prince of Purpoole would almost certainly have sat on the stage. We can picture him seated under a canopy, on a throne bearing his arms, together with his train and his guests. 'Lords, Ladies, and worshipful Personages, that did expect some notable Performance at that time' are there, 'which, indeed, had been effected, if the multitude of Beholders had not been so exceeding great, that thereby there was no convenient room for those that were Actors'. There may well have been a press, for in term the students numbered about 330, and in vacation about 220; and then the guests.

The 'Scaffolds . . . reared to the top of the House' would presumably be tiered seating at the sides of the hall, the tables having been removed, and between the scaffolds a space to be used for dancing or other purposes. On 20 December the Prince's Champion rode the length of the hall on a horse (?hobby-horse), and the Prince, accompanied by more than a hundred people, marched to his throne.

Instead of the houses at the back of the stage, Walter Hodges sees a curtain with enough room behind it for movement from one side to the other (illustration 8). A single door, carried on and off the stage by attendants, is held at a right angle to the front, so that spectators see clearly what is happening on both sides. Perhaps, as the scene requires, the edge of the door carries some sign (cross or phoenix or porcupine?) which tells us whose house we are seeing. People are standing in front of the stage, or sitting on the floor or on stools or benches; as in the previous reconstruction, the Prince and his following sit on the stage. For lighting there are chandeliers, and there may be torch-bearers. In illustration 8 Mr Hodges gives only the essentials: to the left Dromio of Syracuse, within, is challenging and abusing those who are without; behind him Luce is ready to speak and Adriana is emerging from the curtain at the back, while others are grouped behind Dromio; at the right are the angry Ephesian pair, and behind them Angelo and Balthasar. The Prince watches from his throne.

This attractive suggestion is consistent with age-long stage practices in many countries – China and Japan, for example. It perhaps receives support from some words of Sir Philip Sidney:[1] 'VVhat childe is there, that comming to a Play, and seeing *Thebes* written in great Letters vpon an olde doore, doth beleeue that it is *Thebes*?' But we cannot be sure whether the child saw an old door that was carried on to the stage or a door that was stationary at the back of the stage.

Mr Hodges's method of presentation would be very effective in 3.1, where an altercation is actually taking place on both sides of a door; the audience would, as in illustration 8, see both of the Dromios as, unseen to each other, they bandy insults; they would also see the entry, within rather than above, of Luce and Adriana, who would remain invisible to the group outside. It would not, I think, be so satisfactory in certain other parts of the play. In the last scene, for example, there is a good deal of coming and going in and out of the priory (with such explicit stage directions as *Exeunt to the Priorie*

---

[1] Edward Arber (ed.), *Sir Philip Sidney. An Apologie for Poetrie 1595*, 1868, p. 52.

8 Act 3, Scene 1: at the door of Antipholus's house: a conjectural reconstruction of the Gray's Inn performance, 28 December 1594, by C. Walter Hodges

and *Exit one to the Abbesse*), and, as in the preceding scene, much movement and some scuffling among quite a large number of people; a door across the stage would surely be in the way, and would also impede the Prince's view. In 4.1 we also have directions which indicate specific points of entry: *Enter Antipholus Ephes. Dromio from the Courtizans* (13), and *Enter Dromio Sira. from the Bay* (85). And in 3.2 it seems reasonable to suppose that Antipholus of Syracuse and Luciana would enter through the door of the house in which they had just dined together, and that Dromio would escape from Luce through the same door. Other scenes, such as 1.1 and 1.2, would not be helped by a precise indication of their locality. Of the stage sets that I have described I favour those which have three adjoining houses at the back of the stage, and exits to (or from) the bay and the city. Naturally I give precedence to my own version.

The *Gesta*, describing what happened 'at Night' on that Innocents' Day, tells us that 'a Comedy of Errors (like to *Plautus* his *Menechmus*) was played by the Players'; at the 'inquest' on the following night these players are (as part of the joke) referred to as 'base and common Fellows' – the sort of term the grand young gentlemen of the Inn might, but not seriously, apply to professional actors. It has been assumed that these players were the Chamberlain's Men, but here we have a problem. This company is entered in the Chamber Accounts as having been paid for a performance to the Court at Greenwich on Innocents' Day 1594.[1] Chambers, followed by Foakes (p. 116), thought that there could have been a mistake in the Accounts, and that 27 (not 28) December must have been meant, for the company could not have played at Greenwich and at Gray's Inn on the same day.[2] I am not convinced by their belief. A solution to the problem is possibly to be found in a work by Mrs Stopes,[3] who observed that the words 'at night' normally used in the Accounts for payments to players are on this occasion omitted. It is not difficult to accept that the company played at Greenwich in the afternoon and at Gray's Inn late in the evening, perhaps acting the same play on both occasions.

Knapp and Kobialka assume that the 'Players' of the *Gesta* account were members of the Inn. It seems more likely that, as they are referred to in this account, 'those that were Actors' were members who had prepared an entertainment 'to be performed for the Delight of the Beholders', but were unable to present it by reason of the 'disordered Tumult and Crowd upon the Stage'; that, after a period of such 'Sports' as 'Dancing and Revelling with Gentlewomen', probably in the body of the hall, there was reasonable order once more, and a clear stage, and the 'Players', the Chamberlain's Men, who had been engaged to appear, and for whom an appropriate stage was ready in a hall with which they might well have been acquainted, were able to perform their 'Comedy of Errors'. With such a short play the performance could well have been over not much later than midnight. The account of the 'inquest', a tissue of jests, does not bear out the suggestion, tentatively offered by Mr Hodges, that the 'Company of base and common Fellows' were hastily summoned late in the evening 'to make up our Disorders'.

Still in the realms of conjecture, we turn to costumes. There exists a drawing (?1594 or 1595) by Henry Peacham of a scene (not very accurately pictured) in *Titus Andronicus*;

[1] Chambers, *WS*, II, 319.
[2] The Accounts record for this 28 December a payment also to the Admiral's Men.
[3] Charlotte Carmichael Stopes, *The Life of Henry, Earl of Southampton, Shakespeare's Patron*, 1922, p. 73.

9   George Vining and J. Nelson as Antipholus of Syracuse and Antipholus of Ephesus, Princess's Theatre, 1864

the principal men, Titus and two of Tamora's sons, are dressed in what we must take to be an Elizabethan idea of Roman clothes; Tamora and Aaron and two attendants are in Elizabethan garments – which it is thought was the normal practice, whatever the period in which a play was set. Had the players on that evening of Innocents' Day worn anything out of the ordinary, anything other than Elizabethan clothes, we could expect to have been told so in that detailed account of the 'Law-sports, concerning the Night of Errors'. There are elements in our comedy that recall *Commedia dell'Arte* performances. Mr Hodges thinks that the players might have worn clothes similar to those used in *Commedia* presentations; this is an interesting speculation, but it cannot be substantiated.

Stage history

The first known performance of *The Comedy of Errors*, at Gray's Inn, has already been noted (p. 20 above); it took place in 1594.[1] Ten years later, again on Innocents' Day, it was played as part of the Christmas festivities at Court. There follows a long gap in its history on the stage, but some early references to it have come down to us. It is listed among Shakespeare's comedies in Francis Meres's *Palladis Tamia* of 1598, and *The Shakespeare Allusion-Book*[2] records a number of seventeenth-century allusions, but from this century we hear of no productions later than 1604.

In the eighteenth century there were several adaptations, all retaining the main feature of twins faced with strange encounters, but all departing, each in its own way, from the original. The first seems to have been the farce *Every Body Mistaken* of 1716. In October 1734 a comedy in two acts, 'taken from Plautus and Shakespeare' and entitled *See if You Like it, or 'Tis All a Mistake*, was acted at Drury Lane, and was played fairly often at Covent Garden – with variants – for the next seventy or eighty years, and sometimes again at Drury Lane. The most popular adaptation, containing songs and other extra matter, and attributed to the actor and playwright Thomas Hull, was *The Twins, or The Comedy of Errors* (1762); it is more likely that an altered version of 1779 and another of 1793 were by Hull. In these re-creations the play was year after year performed at Covent Garden.[3]

Among versions which did not long hold the stage, there was W. Woods's farce *The Twins, or Which is Which?*, produced in 1780 in Edinburgh and as a three-acter in 1790 at Covent Garden. In J. P. Kemble's adaptation of Hull (printed 1811), which kept the additional scenes and songs, Egeon was almost always played by Hull himself. 'In general, the aim of these versions was to remove, or to conceal, the "improbability" of the events, and to get rid of some of the verbal witticism which amused Georgian audiences less than it had amused Elizabethan.'[4] It is possible that Frederick Reynolds's conversion of the play into an opera (1819) enjoyed as great a success as Kemble's adaptation.[5]

---

[1] See Appendix 1, pp. 111–12 below.

[2] *The Shakespeare Allusion-Book, 1591–1700*, ed. by C. M. Ingleby as *Shakespeare's Centurie of Prayse . . . 1591–1693* (1874); rev. and enlarged by L. T. Smith (1879) and F. J. Furnivall (1886); under its present title by J. Munro (1909); finally re-ed. E. K. Chambers (1932).

[3] See Hogan for these and other eighteenth-century productions.   [4] Harold Child, in NS, p. 117.

[5] Fuller accounts of production in the late eighteenth and the nineteenth centuries are given by Odell.

10 Charles and Henry Webb as Dromio of Syracuse and Dromio of Ephesus, Princess's Theatre, 1864

In 1855 Samuel Phelps brought Shakespeare's *Comedy of Errors* back to the stage (as he did others of the plays), placing it in a double bill with A. R. Slous's *Hamilton of Bothwellhaugh*; in the following year he gave Shakespeare, not Slous, pride of place. Ten years later, as part of the Shakespeare Tercentenary celebrations in 1864, the play was produced at the Princess's Theatre and in provincial towns with two Irish brothers, Charles and Henry Webb, as the Dromios, and George Vining and J. Nelson as the Antipholuses (under the direction of Falconer and Chatterton). A generation later came Sir Frank Benson's London production of 1905, with Benson himself as Antipholus of Syracuse. Sir Philip Ben Greet's 1915 presentation at the Old Vic was notable for one of Sybil Thorndike's earliest appearances – as Adriana – on the London stage. When the play was again seen at the Old Vic in 1927, there was much rumbustious clowning, and the twins wore false noses, two turned up and two turned down. In a Regent's Park production in 1934 *The Comedy of Errors* was, strangely to my mind, paired with *Comus*.

The most famous and probably the most influential mid-century production was Theodor Komisarjevsky's brilliantly farcical burlesque, presented in the Stratford season of 1938 and revived in the following year. Among the comic devices, Komisarjevsky dressed his characters in costumes of many styles and periods, giving most of the men bowler hats of various colours. 'The emphasis was on fun, and the citizens of Ephesus burst into song or moved into ballet whenever tedium threatened.'[1] The music was from Handel and Anthony Bernard. Although some reviewers thought that Komisarjevsky had too grossly traduced Shakespeare, audiences were enthusiastic. He was followed or paralleled in the use of music by several directors; there was, for example, the popular American musical comedy, *The Boys from Syracuse*, first seen in New York in 1938, and later filmed.

There were many other transformations: in 1940 at the Mercury Theatre as a modern-dress amalgam of Plautus, Shakespeare, and Molière, entitled *A New Comedy of Errors, or Too Many Twins*; in 1951 in Cambridge as a musical comedy in the Victorian manner; in 1952 in Canterbury and London with Edwardian costumes, music by Sullivan, and an early-twentieth-century setting in the Near East; in 1954 as a television operetta which two years later was played in London; and in 1965 at Oxford, again as a musical, against a New Orleans waterside background.

During this fun period *The Comedy of Errors* was also several times presented 'seriously', more closely following the play as Shakespeare wrote it: by the Birmingham Repertory Theatre, directed by Douglas Seale, in 1948; by the Bristol Old Vic, directed by Denis Carey, in 1953; by the London Old Vic, directed by Walter Hudd, in 1957. On this last occasion the play was drastically shortened, to be fitted into a double bill with *Titus Andronicus*; Robert Helpmann, miming and gagging the role of Dr Pinch, outshone the rest of the cast.

At short notice, Clifford Williams in 1962 directed a production at Stratford which was so successful that it was revived in the three following seasons; it was taken to America and to Continental countries, including Russia, Finland, and Yugoslavia, and in 1972 was again revived at Stratford. Everywhere it had warm reviews. In *The Times*

[1] Foakes, p. liv.

11   Komisarjevsky's production, Stratford-upon-Avon, 1938: C. Rivers Gadsby as Pinch, Pauline Letts as
Luciana, Valerie Tudor as Adriana

Harold Hobson described it as 'one of the cleverest things Stratford has done for a long time. The wild comedy of irrational recognitions is given consistency and a curious force by the suggestion that there's behind it something vaguely disquieting.' *Izvestia* praised 'the absolute finish and clarity'. Reviewing for the *Guardian*, Michael Billington called Williams's treatment 'a milestone in post-war theatrical production'.

Trevor Nunn's no less popular Stratford production of 1976, after runs at Newcastle and again at Stratford in the following year, was moved to the Aldwych. There were many justly enthusiastic reviews; J. W. Lambert in the *Sunday Times* contrasted Nunn's version with Williams's and described it as 'a bulging basket of song and dance and clowning confrontations'. John Napier's Ephesus 'is the absolute epitome of a timeless Mediterranean tourist trap . . . A lively crowd of tarts, slinky pimps, priests, policemen come and go . . . In pout and patter Judi Dench predictably enchants as the discontented wife; Francesca Annis is a bespectacled delight as her patience-counselling sister, no less flirtatious than reproving.' This production was televised and is available on video-tape.

Another Stratford *Comedy of Errors* was directed by Adrian Noble in 1983. This won praise, but also some adverse criticism for its hotch-potch of comic styles. In the same year there was a BBC television performance on Christmas Eve, its text accompanied by a cast list and a chapter on the production by Henry Fenwick. These days the comedy is often played; it always has been and always will be good theatre.

Text: its nature and origin

For this edition my copy-text has been the 'safe' *Norton Facsimile*[1] ('safe' in that it is made up from pages of the Folio which had been proof-read and corrected in the printing-house), although for the pleasure of handling, I have read the play also in a copy of the Folio in the Cosin Library of the University of Durham.

Nothing suggests that *The Comedy of Errors* was printed earlier than the Folio,[2] in which it stands as the fifth play in the first section, *COMEDIES*, between pages 85 and 100; it is divided into five acts (by whom we do not know), without the scene-divisions of the four plays by which it is preceded. These – *The Tempest, The Two Gentlemen of Verona, The Merry Wives of Windsor*, and *Measure for Measure* – were almost certainly transcripts prepared by the scrivener Ralph Crane for the compositors of the Folio;[3] they contain comparatively few textual irregularities – many, no doubt, were smoothed by Crane.

In contrast with its predecessors in the Folio, *The Comedy of Errors* has many irregularities. Greg (*SF*, p. 201) speaks of 'the extraordinary confusion and inconsistency of the character names and prefixes that persist through most of the play'. To one of the inconsistencies reference has already been made (p. 8 above): the use in entry directions, down to 2.2, of *Erotes* and *Errotis* for Antipholus of Syracuse, of *Sereptus* for Antipholus of

[1] *The Norton Facsimile: The First Folio of Shakespeare*, prepared by Charlton Hinman, New York, 1968.

[2] It is among the sixteen plays entered in the Stationers' Register on 8 November 1623 for 'Mr Blounte [and] Isaak Iaggard'; this supports the view that it was not printed earlier.

[3] F. P. Wilson, 'Ralph Crane, Scrivener to the King's Players', *The Library* VII (1926), 194–215. Compare Greg, *SF*, pp. 100, 217.

12   Clifford Williams's production, Stratford-upon-Avon, 1962: Ian Richardson as Antipholus of Ephesus and Ian Hewitson as Dromio of Ephesus

13   Clifford Williams's production, Stratford-upon-Avon, 1962: James Booth as Pinch, Diana Rigg as Adriana, Ian Richardson as Antipholus of Ephesus and Ian Hewitson as Dromio of Ephesus

14 Trevor Nunn's production, Newcastle, Stratford-upon-Avon and the Aldwych, 1976–7: Judi Dench as Adriana, Francesca Annis (with glasses) as Luciana, Michael Williams as Dromio of Ephesus and Mike Gwilym as Antipholus of Ephesus

Ephesus (in 1.2 *Enter Antipholis Erotes* and in 2.2 *Enter Antipholis Errotis*; in 2.1 *Enter Adriana, wife to Antipholis Sereptus*). We note in passing that in the first two acts the name in the directions is *Antipholis*, thereafter *Antipholus* – the form also used (either by Shakespeare, a scribe, or the compositor) in speeches from 2.2 onwards. Also in the first two acts, once we know which Antipholus is which, *Ant.* is sufficient for speech headings; but from 3.1 onwards, as the confusions increase, the brothers are distinguished by the letters *E.* and *S.* or by their places of origin, *Ephesus, Ephes., Siracusia*; the Dromios are similarly distinguished by letters or abbreviations of the same kind.

Other inconsistencies and complexities attend the characters called 'merchants' in the play. In the entry direction of 1.1 Egeon appears as *the Merchant of Siracusa*, and in the speech headings of this scene as *Marchant, Mer.*, and *Merch.* (We notice that Egeon's name, like that of the Duke, Solinus, is never used except in speeches.) In the second scene there appears another merchant, this time of Ephesus; his speech headings are first *Mer.*, and then *E. Mar.* In Acts 3 and 4 there is yet another merchant, *Balthaser* in the entry direction, *Balthazar* in speeches; his speech headings vary between *Bal., Baltz., Balth., Mar.* (Happily, the merchants are not on the stage as perplexing as they could well have been to the compositor.) In the final scene Balthasar and Egeon have to be on the stage at the same time. Since Balthasar is *Mar.*, Egeon's speech headings must be modified, and so he becomes variously *Mar. Fat., Fa., Fath.*, and *Father*. These are the kinds of inconsistency which, had a transcript or a prompt-book provided the copy, we should have expected to be set right. There is similar diversity in the speech headings of other characters.

The entry direction of 3.2 provides an aberration of a different type. Here we find *Iuliana* where we ought to have *Luciana* (thus corrected in the Second Folio). Her first speech heading is *Iulia.*; elsewhere throughout the play it is *Luc.* or *Luci.* Who was responsible for the error? Then there are Luce and Nell, both of them, surely, the globular kitchen-girl who plays a part in the lives of both Dromios. Was the name Luce changed to Nell in order to make the pun 'an ell' at 3.2.100?

There are stage directions which are fuller than a prompter would need: at the beginning of 2.1, *Enter Adriana, wife to Antipholis Sereptus, with Luciana her sister*, at 4.4.34, *Enter . . . a Schoolmaster, call'd Pinch*, where the information about Pinch's calling is superfluous and not used later – in the dialogue he is never anything but a conjurer. Then we have at 4.4.100 *Enter three or four, and offer to binde him. Hee striues*; at 4.4.140 *Runne all out, as fast as may be, frighted*; at 5.1.407, irregular rather than elaborate, *Exeunt omnes. Manet the two Dromios and two Brothers*. In the second of these three examples it is not quite, in fact, *Exeunt omnes*, for the Syracusan pair remain to comment, with relief and amusement, on the mad rush to escape.

There is a further anomaly at 4.4.140. At the bottom of the first column of page 96 in the Folio:

> *Luc.* God for thy mercy, they are loose againe.
> *Adr.* And come with naked swords,
>   Let's call more helpe to haue them bound againe.
>   *Runne all out.*

At the top of the second column:

> *Off.* Away, they'l kill vs.
>   *Exeunt omnes, as fast as may be, frighted.*

Why this duplication? Carelessness on the part of Shakespeare, or haste, or anxiety to take the play as soon as possible to his company? As Ben Jonson was told by the players, and as we know from *Julius Caesar* and other plays, he did not always correct what he had written. Greg's suggestion (*SF*, p. 201) that a prompter could have been responsible does not convince.

All the inconsistencies, aberrations, and anomalies here listed seem to point to the same conclusion. Many would have been eliminated by a sagacious scribe such as Crane showed himself to be, or by the prompter, whose influence on the text Greg at times suspects.

However, Greg himself finally says, 'In the case of an early play that must have come to the Chamberlain's men from some other company it is, of course, particularly dangerous to dogmatize, but the manuscript behind F was clearly the author's.' This is a conclusion with which we must surely agree.

In the Folio the play is divided into five acts. There are no scene headings, although the act headings, apart from the second (*Actus Secundus*), use the formula *Actus primus, Scena prima* (for the last two acts *Scæna*). I have used the scene-divisions introduced by Rowe in

1709 and followed since his time. I have modernised the spelling and have followed modern usage in punctuation. The Folio stage directions and speech headings are inconsistent; here they are regularised. Additions and alterations to the Folio directions which are required for clarity are enclosed in square brackets. The collation records only such variants and emendations as seem necessary to correct or illuminate the Folio text. References and abbreviations are listed at pp. x–xiii above.

The Comedy of Errors

LIST OF CHARACTERS

SOLINUS, *Duke of Ephesus*
EGEON, *a merchant of Syracuse*
ANTIPHOLUS OF EPHESUS
ANTIPHOLUS OF SYRACUSE } *twin sons of Egeon and Æmilia*
DROMIO OF EPHESUS
DROMIO OF SYRACUSE } *twin slaves of the Antipholuses*
BALTHASAR, *a merchant*
ANGELO, *a goldsmith*
DOCTOR PINCH, *a schoolmaster (or conjurer)*
FIRST MERCHANT
SECOND MERCHANT
An OFFICER
A JAILER
A MESSENGER

ÆMILIA, *wife of Egeon and Abbess of the Priory in Ephesus*
ADRIANA, *wife of Antipholus of Ephesus*
LUCIANA, *Adriana's sister*
LUCE (*or* NELL), *Adriana's kitchen-maid*
A COURTESAN

Officers, Headsman, Attendants

THE COMEDY OF ERRORS

1.1 *Enter* [SOLINUS,] *the Duke of Ephesus, with* [EGEON,] *the merchant of Syracuse,* JAILER, *and other attendants*

EGEON Proceed, Solinus, to procure my fall,
And by the doom of death end woes and all.
DUKE Merchant of Syracusa, plead no more.
I am not partial to infringe our laws.
The enmity and discord which of late   5
Sprung from the rancorous outrage of your Duke
To merchants, our well-dealing countrymen,
Who, wanting guilders to redeem their lives,
Have sealed his rigorous statutes with their bloods,
Excludes all pity from our threatening looks.   10
For since the mortal and intestine jars

Act 1, Scene 1 Title] The Comedie of Errors. F *(ital. in running headlines)* 1.1] *Actus primus, Scena prima.* F 0 SD]
Enter the Duke of Ephesus, with the Merchant of Siracusa, Iaylor, and other attendants. F 1 SH EGEON] *Marchant.* F *(printed
above the line; elsewhere in scene / Mer. / or / Merch.)*

Act 1, Scene 1
1.1 F has the sub-heading *Actus primus, Scena prima.* All five acts are similarly headed, but no scene-divisions are provided. This edition gives the scene-divisions which have become traditional since Rowe added them in 1709.
As is implied throughout, the action of the entire play, in the fashion of Roman comedy, takes place in the open, here the mart, or market-place, of Ephesus. Facing us are three 'houses': that in the centre, which represents the priory, is marked with a cross or other religious symbol; this is flanked on the one side by the house of Antipholus of Ephesus, marked with the sign of a Phoenix, on the other side by the house of the Courtesan, marked with the sign of a Porcupine. (See the section on staging, pp. 21–3 above.)
1 **Proceed** This, and 'plead no more' (3), imply that the action begins *in media re*. The scene as a whole serves the purpose of a prologue, and in addition, together with the final scene, provides an 'envelope' within which the farcical section of the play is enclosed.
2 **doom** sentence, judgement.

4 **partial** inclined, apt. *OED* notes that this sense of the word is obsolete.
6 **outrage** violence; as at 4.4.110.
8 **wanting guilders** lacking money. A guilder was '(a) a gold coin formerly current in the Netherlands and parts of Germany; (b) a Dutch silver coin worth about 1s 8d English' (*OED*). Shakespeare uses the word only in this play, apparently with the general sense of 'money'.
8 **redeem** ransom.
9 **sealed ... bloods** ratified his severe laws with their lives. The colour of blood is perhaps intended to echo the colour suggested by the red of sealing-wax.
10 **Excludes** So far separated from the double subject in 5, the singular is acceptable Shakespearean usage; see Abbott 336.
11 **intestine jars** deadly quarrels. 'Intestine' is here synonymous with, and intensifies, 'mortal'; compare *1H4* 1.1.12: 'the intestine shock / And furious close of civil butchery'. The alternative meaning 'internal' is also implied, suggesting a form of civil war between two Greek city-states.

41

'Twixt thy seditious countrymen and us
It hath in solemn synods been decreed
Both by the Syracusians and ourselves
To admit no traffic to our adverse towns.   15
Nay, more: if any born at Ephesus
Be seen at Syracusian marts and fairs;
Again, if any Syracusian born
Come to the bay of Ephesus, he dies,
His goods confiscate to the Duke's dispose,   20
Unless a thousand marks be levièd
To quit the penalty and to ransom him.
Thy substance, valued at the highest rate,
Cannot amount unto a hundred marks;
Therefore by law thou art condemned to die.   25
EGEON Yet this my comfort: when your words are done,
My woes end likewise with the evening sun.
DUKE Well, Syracusian, say in brief the cause
Why thou departed'st from thy native home,
And for what cause thou cam'st to Ephesus.   30
EGEON A heavier task could not have been imposed
Than I to speak my griefs unspeakable.
Yet, that the world may witness that my end
Was wrought by nature, not by vile offence,
I'll utter what my sorrow gives me leave.   35
In Syracusa was I born, and wed

17 at Syracusian] *Pope;* at any Siracusian F

13 **synods** councils, legislative assemblies.
15 To allow no trade between our hostile towns. A common meaning of 'traffic' in Shakespeare (e.g. *Shr.* 1.1.12, *WT* 4.3.23).
17 **Be . . . marts** In the F reading, 'Be seene at any *Siracusian* marts', the 'any' is seen by most editors as an intrusion picked up from the previous and following lines, and is omitted, the metre being thus regularised, as here. Malone took 'Nay more' as a separate interjectional line, and retained 'any' in 17. Riverside raises 'be seen' to the previous line, making it a hexameter, and retains 'any' in 17.
17 **marts** markets.
20 **confiscate** forfeited (past participle, with accent on the second syllable; but at 1.2.2 the accent is on the first syllable).
20 **dispose** disposal.
21 **marks** There was no coin so named. Mark

was a denomination of weight, formerly employed (chiefly for gold and silver) throughout western Europe. In England its value was early fixed at 13*s* 4*d*, or two-thirds of the pound sterling (*OED*). As in his use of 'guilder', Shakespeare is probably not thinking in such precise terms, but naming a sum which to his English audience would represent a considerable amount of money.
22 **quit the penalty** pay the fine.
27 **evening sun** Like 150–4, these lines establish the time-span of the action as a single day.
31–2 **A heavier task . . . unspeakable** A clear echo of Virgil, *Aeneid* 11.3: *infandum, regina, iubes renovare dolorem.* Quasi-proverbial by the sixteenth century. See Tilley R89.
34 **wrought by nature** brought about by natural affection – his love for his son.

Unto a woman happy but for me,
And by me, had not our hap been bad.
With her I lived in joy, our wealth increased
By prosperous voyages I often made   40
To Epidamnum, till my factor's death,
And the great care of goods at random left,
Drew me from kind embracements of my spouse,
From whom my absence was not six months old
Before herself (almost at fainting under   45
The pleasing punishment that women bear)
Had made provision for her following me,
And soon and safe arrivèd where I was.
There had she not been long but she became
A joyful mother of two goodly sons;   50
And, which was strange, the one so like the other
As could not be distinguished but by names.
That very hour, and in the self-same inn,
A mean woman was deliverèd
Of such a burden male, twins both alike.   55
Those, for their parents were exceeding poor,
I bought, and brought up to attend my sons.

41 Epidamnum] *Pope;* Epidamium F *(throughout scene)*   42 the great care ... at random left,] *Theobald;* he great
care ... at randone left, F; he great store ... at randone leaving, F2   54 mean] meane F; poor meane F2; poor mean
Malone; meaner *Walker*   55 burden male, twins] burthen Male, twins F; burthen Maletwins F2

37–8 happy ... bad Perhaps best
paraphrased, 'happy alone in (possessing) me,
and through me as well, had we not been
unfortunate'. To gloss 'but' as 'except', as some
editors do, seems inadmissible in the light of the
following line.

38 hap fortune; with a wry pun on 'happy' (37).

38 The line is often said to be short by a syllable, and some editors adopt the unauthoritative
F2 reading, 'by me too' (e.g. NS, Wells).
However, short lines are common in Shakespeare
(e.g. 54 in the present scene); compare Abbott
508, where antithesis is noted as one reason for
the occurrence of such lines. This line is
rendered metrically acceptable if 'And' is
stressed.

41 Epidamnum The form used by Plautus,
followed by Warner, as a setting for *Menaechmi*.
The Greek form was Epidamnos. The Romans
changed the name to Dyrrachium. F consistently
spells the name *Epidamium*. According to T. W.
Baldwin in his American Arden (1928), early editions of Plautus sometimes read 'Epidamnium',
and it is possible that Shakespeare used this form,

which by minim misreading became Epidamium
in F.

41 factor agent.

42 care of concern about.

42 at random untended, neglected.

43 kind loving, affectionate.

52 distinguished ... names To help to bring
about the errors of the play, the two pairs of
identical twins are given identical names (see 128
and n., and p. 7 above). However, on their first
notice in entry SDS Antipholus of Syracuse is
named 'Antipholis Erotes' (? the wandering twin,
from Latin *errare*; ? confusion with the
Courtesan's name, Erotium, in Plautus); Antipholus of Ephesus is 'Antipholis Sereptus' (*surreptus* = snatched away). See 2.1.0 SD. In Plautus
they are Sosicles and Menaechmus (Menechmus
in Warner's translation).

54 mean Malone, without authority,
regularised the metre with 'poor mean', and
W. S. Walker, in his *Critical Examination*, with
'meaner'. Such regularisation is unwarranted.
See 38 n. 'Mean' (= of poor social standing) is
recalled at 58 by 'meanly' (= to no small degree).

My wife, not meanly proud of two such boys,
Made daily motions for our home return.
Unwilling I agreed. Alas, too soon   60
We came aboard.
A league from Epidamnum had we sailed
Before the always-wind-obeying deep
Gave any tragic instance of our harm.
But longer did we not retain much hope,   65
For what obscurèd light the heavens did grant
Did but convey unto our fearful minds
A doubtful warrant of immediate death,
Which though myself would gladly have embraced,
Yet the incessant weepings of my wife,   70
Weeping before for what she saw must come,
And piteous plainings of the pretty babes,
That mourned for fashion, ignorant what to fear,
Forced me to seek delays for them and me.
And this it was (for other means was none):   75
The sailors sought for safety by our boat,
And left the ship, then sinking-ripe, to us.
My wife, more careful for the latter-born,
Had fastened him unto a small spare mast
Such as seafaring men provide for storms.   80
To him one of the other twins was bound,
Whilst I had been like heedful of the other.
The children thus disposed, my wife and I,
Fixing our eyes on whom our care was fixed,
Fastened ourselves at either end the mast,   85
And floating straight, obedient to the stream,
Was carried towards Corinth, as we thought.

60–1] *Lineation as Pope; single line* F   75] F4; And this it was: (for other meanes was none) F

59 motions entreaties, urgings.
  61 we came aboard F prints this as part of the preceding line. NS unnecessarily feels that the irregularity 'suggests a "cut"'. Other editors (e.g. Cuningham) also suspect a hiatus. But broken lines are frequent in Shakespeare (see Abbott 511–12), and, as here, can be expressive.
  63 always-wind-obeying An early example of Shakespeare's recognition of the real and symbolic power of the wind over human destinies (as in *Twelfth Night*, *The Tempest*, and *Pericles*).
  64 tragic instance ominous sign.

  68 doubtful warrant frightening assurance; compare *MV* 3.2.109: 'doubtful thoughts, and rash-embrac'd despair'.
  73 for fashion in a similar way.
  74 delays delays from perishing.
  75 this it was thus it came about.
  78 latter-born See 124 n.
  84 on whom on those on whom.
  86 straight straightway.
  87 Was Another example of a singular verb with a double subject; compare 10 n.

At length the sun, gazing upon the earth,
Dispersed those vapours that offended us,
And by the benefit of his wished light   90
The seas waxed calm, and we discoverèd
Two ships from far, making amain to us:
Of Corinth that, of Epidaurus this.
But ere they came – O, let me say no more.
Gather the sequel by that went before.   95

DUKE Nay, forward, old man; do not break off so,
For we may pity, though not pardon thee.

EGEON O, had the gods done so, I had not now
Worthily termed them merciless to us;
For ere the ships could meet by twice five leagues   100
We were encountered by a mighty rock,
Which being violently borne upon,
Our helpful ship was splitted in the midst;
So that in this unjust divorce of us
Fortune had left to both of us alike   105
What to delight in, what to sorrow for.
Her part, poor soul, seeming as burdenèd
With lesser weight but not with lesser woe,
Was carried with more speed before the wind,
And in our sight they three were taken up   110
By fishermen of Corinth, as we thought.
At length another ship had seized on us,
And, knowing whom it was their hap to save,
Gave healthful welcome to their shipwracked guests,
And would have reft the fishers of their prey   115
Had not their bark been very slow of sail;

93 Epidaurus] Epidarus F   94 came – O, let … more] *Pope;* came, oh let … more F   102 upon,] *Pope;* vp, F
103 helpful] helpefull F; helpless *Rowe*   116 bark] F2; backe F

89 **vapours … offended** mists (or clouds)
that assailed.

90 **by the benefit** by the agency.

92 **amain** at speed.

93 **Epidaurus** The description of the drifting
of the mast suggests that Shakespeare had in
mind, not the Epidaurus in Argolis, famed for its
temple of Aesculapius, but the Epidaurus on the
Adriatic coast, formerly Ragusa and now
Dubrovnik.

99 **Worthily** Rightly.

103 **helpful ship** i.e. the mast, which was
indeed proving helpful. Rowe's emendation

'helpless' is not nearly so appropriate.

103 **splitted** A not uncommon form; compare
5.1.308, *2H6* 3.2.411, *Ant.* 5.1.24.

111 **as we thought** Egeon does not yet know
where his lost wife, son, and servant were
conveyed.

114 **shipwracked** Shakespeare invariably uses
the spelling 'wrack', retained by Riverside, and
recorded in the *Harvard Concordance*.

116 **bark** This, the F2 reading, is an obvious
compositorial correction of the F 'backe'. It is
possible to misread *r* as *c* in English Secretary
hand.

And therefore homeward did they bend their course.
Thus have you heard me severed from my bliss,
That by misfortunes was my life prolonged
To tell sad stories of my own mishaps.   120
DUKE   And for the sake of them thou sorrow'st for,
Do me the favour to dilate at full
What have befall'n of them and thee till now.
EGEON   My youngest boy, and yet my eldest care,
At eighteen years became inquisitive   125
After his brother, and importuned me
That his attendant, so his case was like,
Reft of his brother, but retained his name,
Might bear him company in the quest of him;
Whom whilst I laboured of a love to see,   130
I hazarded the loss of whom I loved.
Five summers have I spent in farthest Greece,
Roaming clean through the bounds of Asia,
And coasting homeward came to Ephesus,
Hopeless to find, yet loath to leave unsought   135
Or that or any place that harbours men.
But here must end the story of my life,
And happy were I in my timely death
Could all my travels warrant me they live.
DUKE   Hapless Egeon, whom the fates have marked   140
To bear the extremity of dire mishap!

123 thee] F2; they F

122–3 We may compare with Egeon's sad story and the poignant part played in it by 'hap', 'mishap', 'gods', and 'fate' the Chorus-narrations in *Pericles*.

122 **dilate at full** relate in detail.

123 **What have befall'n** For a comparable false concord, compare 87 above and the numerous examples in Abbott 333.

124 **My youngest boy** In 78 we are told that the mother took the 'latter-born'. The inconsistency in detail, of a kind not uncommon in Shakespeare, is not likely to be noticed in the theatre.

127 **so . . . like** so similar was his case.

128 **retained his name** 'retained' = 'having retained' – another inconsistency; see 52 n. We can accept that, in order to multiply the confusions of the play, Shakespeare caused the boy and his attendant who were saved with the father to assume the names of their twins. He follows Plautus in this, except that Plautus has only the merchant's twin sons, and no equivalent to the Dromios.

130–1 While I strove out of my love to see him (the lost twin), I risked the loss of the other whom I (also) loved.

132–4 In *Menaechmi* (234–8) Messenio says, 'This is the sixth year that we've been on this job. Istrians, Spaniards, Massilians, Illyrians, the whole of the upper sea [Adriatic] and foreign Greece [Magna Graecia], and all the coasts of Italy – whatever shores are washed by the sea – we've been round the lot.' Shakespeare substitutes Asia for most of these names, since he has made Ephesus his setting. Foakes suggests that he 'may have had in mind also the travels of St Paul; compare Acts 19.1: "Paul when he passed through the upper coastes, came to Ephesus".' We may note three aspects of the voyage: a human quest, a surrender to chance, and a knowing or unknowing pilgrimage.

133 **bounds** territories.

Now trust me, were it not against our laws,
Against my crown, my oath, my dignity,
Which princes, would they, may not disannul,
My soul should sue as advocate for thee.   145
But though thou art adjudgèd to the death,
And passèd sentence may not be recalled
But to our honour's great disparagement,
Yet will I favour thee in what I can.
Therefore, merchant, I'll limit thee this day   150
To seek thy health by beneficial help.
Try all the friends thou hast in Ephesus;
Beg thou or borrow to make up the sum,
And live. If no, then thou art doomed to die.
Jailer, take him to thy custody.   155

JAILER I will, my lord.
EGEON Hopeless and helpless doth Egeon wend,
But to procrastinate his lifeless end.

Exeunt

1.2 *Enter* ANTIPHOLUS [OF SYRACUSE, FIRST] MERCHANT, *and*
DROMIO [OF SYRACUSE]

1 MERCHANT Therefore give out you are of Epidamnum
Lest that your goods too soon be confiscate.
This very day a Syracusian merchant
Is apprehended for arrival here,

143–4] *As in* F; *lines transposed by Theobald*   151 health] *NS;* helpe F   157 Egeon] *Egean* F   158 lifeless] liuelesse
F   Act 1, Scene 2   1.2] *Pope; not in* F   0 SD] *Enter Antipholis Erotes, a Marchant, and Dromio.* F   1 SH] 1 MERCHANT]
Mer. F *(at 24 and 32 / E. Mar)*   1 Epidamnum] *Pope; Epidamium* F   4 arrival] F2; a riuall F

143 **dignity** high office.
144 **would they** even if they wished.
144 **disannul** cancel, annul.
147 **recalled** revoked.
150 **limit . . . day** allow you today as your limit.
This again establishes the duration of the action.
151 **health** F reads 'helpe'. The NS emendation to 'health' must surely be accepted. The F error no doubt arose from the compositor's anticipation of 'helpe' as he read the whole line.
158 **procrastinate** postpone. Not found elsewhere in Shakespeare.

Act 1, Scene 2
0 SD Antipholus of Syracuse appears in F as *Antipholis Erotes* (see 1.1.52 n.). The First Mer-

chant appears as *a Marchant*; 'First' is supplied to distinguish this merchant, perhaps a Syracusan who has concealed his place of origin and is accepted in Ephesus (24), from the Merchant who appears in 4.1 and thereafter. The speech headings are discussed at pp. 34–6 above.
1 SH 1 MERCHANT Here F reads *Mer.*; for his two subsequent speeches *E. Mar.* If this is intended to suggest that he is an Ephesian, and not, as conjectured in the previous note, a Syracusan, he presumably has no sympathy with the law prescribing death for visiting Syracusans.
4 **arrival** F2. The F 'a riuall' is paralleled by *Shr.* 4.5.41, 'A lots' for 'Allots'.

And, not being able to buy out his life,   5
According to the statute of the town
Dies ere the weary sun set in the west.
There is your money that I had to keep.
ANTIPHOLUS S. Go, bear it to the Centaur, where we host,
And stay there, Dromio, till I come to thee.   10
Within this hour it will be dinner-time.
Till that I'll view the manners of the town,
Peruse the traders, gaze upon the buildings,
And then return and sleep within mine inn;
For with long travel I am stiff and weary.   15
Get thee away.
DROMIO S. Many a man would take you at your word
And go indeed, having so good a mean.   *Exit*
ANTIPHOLUS S. A trusty villain, sir, that very oft,
When I am dull with care and melancholy,   20
Lightens my humour with his merry jests.
What, will you walk with me about the town,
And then go to my inn and dine with me?
1 MERCHANT I am invited, sir, to certain merchants,
Of whom I hope to make much benefit.   25
I crave your pardon. Soon at five o'clock,
Please you, I'll meet with you upon the mart,
And afterward consort you till bedtime.

9 SH ANTIPHOLUS S.] *Ant.* F *(throughout scene)*   17 SH DROMIO S.] *Dro.* F   18 SD *Exit*] *Exit Dromio* F   26 o'clock] a
clocke F

5 buy out redeem.
9 Centaur The inn at which they are lodging
('host'). Inns, shops, and even some houses were
identified by signs bearing pictures. See the description of a possible stage set at pp. 21–3 above.
11–14 For another passage expressing the
interest that a character takes in a city new to him
compare *TN* 3.3.19–24.
11 dinner-time i.e. shortly before noon, by
which time the meal, if uneaten, was likely to be
burnt or cold (see 44–7); compare the proverb,
represented by many examples in Tilley (s872),
'My stomach has struck twelve.' For another
instance of appetite as a measure of time see 66.
18 And would indeed make off [with the
money], having so good an opportunity. For this
sense of 'mean' compare *The Rape of Lucrece*
1045: 'Some happy mean to end a hapless life'.
The word may also, as Baldwin suggests, be
intended to hold the sense of 'means', as at *MM*
2.2.24: 'Let her have needful but not lavish
means.' *OED* records no earlier example of this

use of the word.
19 villain As often in Shakespeare, used good-
humouredly. NS suggests that it also carries the
sense of villein or bondsman, as in *The Rape of
Lucrece* 1338: 'The homely villain cur'sies to her
low.'
21 humour mood, disposition. The context
implies melancholy, the heaviest and darkest of
the four humours which, in Elizabethan medi-
cine, determine our moods and temperaments;
frequent in Shakespeare – e.g. 'cloudy melancholy' (*Tit.* 2.3.33), 'shade of melancholy boughs'
(*AYLI* 2.7.111). 'Lightens', too, suggests by contrast the hue of 'sable-coloured melancholy . . .
the black oppressing humour' (*LLL* 1.1.231–3).
26 Soon at five o'clock One of several indications of the hour at which the action of the play is
to be completed; compare 1.1.150 and 4.1.10.
26 o'clock F 'a clocke' is the almost universal
form in Shakespeare.
28 consort accompany, attend.

My present business calls me from you now.

ANTIPHOLUS S.　Farewell till then. I will go lose myself　　　　　30
And wander up and down to view the city.

1 MERCHANT　Sir, I commend you to your own content.　　　*Exit*

ANTIPHOLUS S.　He that commends me to mine own content
Commends me to the thing I cannot get.
I to the world am like a drop of water　　　　　　　　　　35
That in the ocean seeks another drop,
Who, falling there to find his fellow forth,
Unseen, inquisitive, confounds himself.
So I, to find a mother and a brother,
In quest of them unhappy, lose myself.　　　　　　　　　　40

　　　　　　Enter DROMIO OF EPHESUS

Here comes the almanac of my true date.
What now? How chance thou art returned so soon?

DROMIO E.　Returned so soon? Rather approached too late.
The capon burns, the pig falls from the spit.
The clock hath strucken twelve upon the bell;　　　　　　45
My mistress made it one upon my cheek.
She is so hot because the meat is cold.
The meat is cold because you come not home.
You come not home because you have no stomach.
You have no stomach, having broke your fast.　　　　　　50
But we that know what 'tis to fast and pray

---

32 SD *Exit*] *Exeunt.* F　　40 unhappy] F2; (vnhappie a) F; unhappier *NS, conj. Clark*

30 lose myself wander about at random (as at 11–14). It may, as also at 40, imply 'lose my wits', in anticipation of the errors and confusions of the day.

35–8 drop . . . himself Foakes suggests that 'this image perhaps grew by association from Egeon's account of his shipwreck, and parallels his story of searching by sea . . . for his lost sons. It is a prominent and potent image in a play much concerned with identity.' We may compare Antony's uncertainty about his own identity (*Ant.* 4.14.9–11).

37 find . . . forth seek out its companion.

38 confounds himself 'mingles indistinguishably' (Onions) with the rest; compare 'lose myself' (30 and n., and 40 below).

40 unhappy unfortunate.

41 almanac In Dromio (it does not matter that it is the wrong Dromio, since he and his brother

were twins, born on the same day as their twin masters) Antipholus of Syracuse sees one of his own age, as in a calendar; one of the 'same term of existence' (Onions) as himself. Compare 5.1.404, 'the calendars of their nativity'.

45 strucken The form is found also at *LLL* 4.3.220 and *JC* 3.1.29 (in both examples spelt 'strooken').

45 twelve See 11 n. above.

46 made it one An obvious play on words: 'made it one o'clock'; 'struck me one blow'.

49 stomach appetite.

51 we . . . pray Here 'pray' seems to have little relevance, except perhaps as a jest on Dromio's part. Did 'fast' possibly awaken in Shakespeare's mind associations with the verse in Mark 9.29, alluding to the casting out of an evil spirit ('This kind can come forth by nothing but by prayer and fasting')?

Are penitent for your default today.

ANTIPHOLUS S. Stop in your wind, sir. Tell me this, I pray:
Where have you left the money that I gave you?

DROMIO E. O, sixpence that I had o' Wednesday last 55
To pay the saddler for my mistress' crupper.
The saddler had it, sir. I kept it not.

ANTIPHOLUS S. I am not in a sportive humour now.
Tell me, and dally not: where is the money?
We being strangers here, how dar'st thou trust 60
So great a charge from thine own custody?

DROMIO E. I pray you, jest, sir, as you sit at dinner.
I from my mistress come to you in post.
If I return I shall be post indeed,
For she will scour your fault upon my pate. 65
Methinks your maw, like mine, should be your clock
And strike you home without a messenger.

ANTIPHOLUS S. Come, Dromio, come, these jests are out of season.
Reserve them till a merrier hour than this.
Where is the gold I gave in charge to thee? 70

DROMIO E. To me, sir? Why, you gave no gold to me.

ANTIPHOLUS S. Come on, sir knave, have done your foolishness,
And tell me how thou hast disposed thy charge.

DROMIO E. My charge was but to fetch you from the mart
Home to your house, the Phoenix, sir, to dinner. 75

64 indeed,] *Capell;* indeed. F   65 scour] scoure F; score *Pope*   66 clock] *Pope;* cooke F

52 **penitent** doing penance – by fasting, as also by suffering punishment.

52 **default** fault, offence.

53 **Stop ... wind** Keep your breath [? your idle chatter] to yourself, hold your tongue.

56 **crupper** The strap which passes from the back of the horse's tail and round its hindquarters (its croup) to stop the saddle from sliding forward.

62 **jest** Each believes the other to be speaking 'in a sportive humour'.

63 **in post** post-haste, like a courier.

64 **post** The door-post in a tavern on which a reckoning was scored.

65 **scour** A play on words: (1) score = mark or notch the tavern-post to keep a reckoning; (2) scour = 'beat, punish' (Onions), as in *H5* 2.1.55: 'I will scour you with my rapier', where the same quibble as in the present passage may be intended.

66 **maw** stomach

66 **clock** Pope's emendation of the F 'cooke' seems safe in the context, and in the light of the proverbial allusion of which Tilley gives several examples under B287a, 'The belly is the truest clock', and elsewhere.

73 **disposed** disposed of, deposited.

75 **Phoenix** The house, or place of business, of Antipholus of Ephesus is marked by the sign of a Phoenix; the name is used several times later (e.g. at 88). As Foakes notes, 'The Phoenix was the sign of a London tavern, and also of a shop in Lombard Street, according to Sugden, *Dictionary*, p. 409. The tavern is referred to in the prologue of Ben Jonson's *Staple of News.*' It seems to me fanciful to suggest, as Foakes does, that the choice of this sign is thematically apt, since, just as the phoenix is reborn from its own ashes, so Antipholus and Adriana rise from their unhappy married life to a new love.

My mistress and her sister stays for you.

ANTIPHOLUS S. Now, as I am a Christian, answer me
In what safe place you have bestowed my money,
Or I shall break that merry sconce of yours
That stands on tricks when I am undisposed.   80
Where is the thousand marks thou hadst of me?

DROMIO E. I have some marks of yours upon my pate,
Some of my mistress' marks upon my shoulders,
But not a thousand marks between you both.
If I should pay your worship those again,   85
Perchance you will not bear them patiently.

ANTIPHOLUS S. Thy mistress' marks? What mistress, slave, hast thou?

DROMIO E. Your worship's wife, my mistress at the Phoenix;
She that doth fast till you come home to dinner,
And prays that you will hie you home to dinner.   90

antipholus s. What, wilt thou flout me thus unto my face,
Being forbid? There, take you that, sir knave.

                    [*He beats Dromio*]

DROMIO E. What mean you, sir? For God's sake hold your hands.
Nay, an you will not, sir, I'll take my heels.   *Exit*

ANTIPHOLUS S. Upon my life, by some device or other   95
The villain is o'er-raught of all my money.
They say this town is full of cozenage,
As nimble jugglers that deceive the eye,
Dark-working sorcerers that change the mind,
Soul-killing witches that deform the body,   100
Disguisèd cheaters, prating mountebanks,
And many suchlike liberties of sin.

93 God's] F3; God F   94 SD *Exit*] F2; *Exeunt Dromio Ep.* F   96 o'er-raught] *Capell;* ore-wrought F   102 liberties] F; libertines *Hanmer*

76 stays A further example of the singular verb form with a compound subject.

77 Christian The period in which the action is set cannot be determined, and needs no discussion; as various references to money make clear (e.g. 'sixpence', 55), Shakespeare is writing as an Elizabethan, and his anachronism here is interesting only as part of his assimilation of a Christian ethos into a 'Roman' comedy.

79 sconce head.

80 stands on engages itself in.

81 thousand marks Antipholus, ironically, since he does not know of his father's presence in Ephesus, has the very sum required to ransom Egeon (1.1.21). The quibbling on 'marks' that

follows emphasises the irony.

85 pay Foakes here notes 'quibbling on the sense "beat, flog"' (*OED* Pay v^7 3c), comparing 4.4.10.

96 The rascal has tricked me out of all my money.

97–105 This is discussed at pp. 7–8 above in relation to the reputation of Ephesus in Elizabethan England.

97 cozenage cheating.

101 prating mountebanks itinerant quack-doctors crying up their so-called remedies.

102 liberties of sin licensed transgressors. Hanmer read 'libertines' for 'liberties'.

If it prove so, I will be gone the sooner.
I'll to the Centaur to go seek this slave.
I greatly fear my money is not safe.   *Exit*   105

2.1 *Enter* ADRIANA, *wife to* ANTIPHOLUS [OF EPHESUS], *with*
LUCIANA, *her sister*

ADRIANA Neither my husband nor the slave returned,
That in such haste I sent to seek his master?
Sure, Luciana, it is two o'clock.
LUCIANA Perhaps some merchant hath invited him,
And from the mart he's somewhere gone to dinner.   5
Good sister, let us dine, and never fret.
A man is master of his liberty;
Time is their master, and when they see time
They'll go or come. If so, be patient, sister.
ADRIANA Why should their liberty than ours be more?   10
luciana Because their business still lies out o'door.
ADRIANA Look, when I serve him so, he takes it ill.
LUCIANA O, know he is the bridle of your will.
ADRIANA There's none but asses will be bridled so.

104 to go] F; go to *Rowe*   **Act 2, Scene 1   2.1**] *Pope; Actus Secundus* F   0 SD] *Enter Adriana, wife to Antipholis Sereptus,*
with Luciana her sister F   3 o'clock] a clocke F   11 o'door] adore F   12 ill] F2; thus F

104 Centaur See 9 n. above.

Act 2, Scene 1
0 SD OF EPHESUS The F *Sereptus* is derived from
Plautus, who in the prologue to *Menaechmi* refers
to the lost twin as *puerum surruptum,* 'the boy who
was snatched away' from his home at Tarentum
as an infant and brought to Epidamnum, and
hence corresponds to Shakespeare's Antipholus
of Ephesus. For more detail see pp. 34–6 above.
   In this scene, as elsewhere, especially 3.2,
Shakespeare's use of rhyme and of swift one-line
exchanges (stichomythia) helps to express the
symmetrical and sharp double-truths with which
the play so often engages.
   3 two o'clock At 1.2.45 it was twelve o'clock.
It is unlikely that the ladies would have waited two
hours before speaking as they now do; nor is it
probable that an audience would make anything
of, or even notice, the discrepancy. Shakespeare
may have intended it to make play with the
domestic tensions created when husbands are late
for dinner.
   7 This has a proverbial ring, but no close paral-

lel is recorded; Tilley's quotations under 'As free
as air' (A88) are perhaps as close as any.
   7–9 As Wells points out, the sequence of
thought in these lines is not clear. Perhaps, says
Wells, Luciana means, 'So far as we are concerned, men will do as they please; but they are
nevertheless subject to the demands of time, and
will come or go as their larger responsibilities
permit.'
   7–25 These lines express an important theme
of the play. See pp. 7, 11 above, where the
influence of Ephesus is discussed. The passage
has also several echoes of the Old Testament.
(See 16–24 n.)
   11 still always
   11 out o'door away from home.
   12 When I treat him as he treats me, he takes it
amiss.
   12 ill F reads 'thus', which the compositor may
subconsciously have picked up from 'so' earlier
in the line. Both sense and the rhyming verse-
pattern make clear that 'thus' is wrong, and
the F2 'ill' seems an obvious correction.

LUCIANA Why, headstrong liberty is lashed with woe.   15
　　　　　There's nothing situate under heaven's eye
　　　　　But hath his bound in earth, in sea, in sky.
　　　　　The beasts, the fishes, and the wingèd fowls
　　　　　Are their males' subjects, and at their controls.
　　　　　Man, more divine, the master of all these,   20
　　　　　Lord of the wide world and wild watery seas,
　　　　　Indued with intellectual sense and souls,
　　　　　Of more pre-eminence than fish and fowls,
　　　　　Are masters to their females, and their lords.
　　　　　Then let your will attend on their accords.   25
ADRIANA This servitude makes you to keep unwed.
LUCIANA Not this, but troubles of the marriage-bed.
ADRIANA But were you wedded, you would bear some sway.
LUCIANA Ere I learn love, I'll practise to obey.
ADRIANA How if your husband start some otherwhere?   30
LUCIANA Till he come home again, I would forbear.
ADRIANA Patience unmoved! No marvel though she pause.
　　　　　They can be meek that have no other cause.
　　　　　A wretched soul, bruised with adversity,
　　　　　We bid be quiet when we hear it cry.   35
　　　　　But were we burdened with like weight of pain,
　　　　　As much or more we should ourselves complain.
　　　　　So thou, that hast no unkind mate to grieve thee,
　　　　　With urging helpless patience would relieve me.

22–3 souls, / . . . fowls,] F; soule, / . . . fowle F2

15 lashed scourged, whipped. This, with the previous line, expresses Luciana's belief that 'headstrong liberty' in a wife is more foolish than accepting the bridle of a husband's authority.

16–24 As Foakes points out, this passage owes much to Gen. 1.25, 28, or Ps. 8.4–8, as well as to the doctrine of Ephes. 5. In Gen. 1 God gives newly-created man dominion over fish, fowls of the air, cattle, and every creeping thing. In Ps. 8 likewise man has been given dominion over all things, and again beasts and fowls and fish are named. Katherina expresses much the same sentiments in *Shr.* 5.2.136–79. In both plays the biblical doctrine is extended from animals to wives, and yields startling, even shocking, domestic comedy.

20–4 Man . . . their lords Note the plural verb and complement, 'Are masters . . . and their lords', and 'souls' (22), after the singular subject 'Man'.

25 accords assent, consent; compare *H5* 5.2.71: 'With full accord to all our just demands'.

28 sway authority

30 start . . . otherwhere sets off in pursuit of some other woman. For this use of 'otherwhere' compare 102.

32 pause i.e. pause to consider before committing herself to marriage. Adriana's use of the third person could suggest that she has all women in mind.

33 cause i.e. no cause to be otherwise.

34–7 Proverbial. See Tilley A124, 'All commend patience, but none can endure to suffer', and compare *Ado* 5.1.35–6: 'For there was never yet philosopher / That could endure the toothache patiently.' The parallel with the present passage is close in other lines in *Ado* (5.1.27–31).

But if thou live to see like right bereft,   40
This fool-begged patience in thee will be left.
LUCIANA   Well, I will marry one day, but to try.
Here comes your man. Now is your husband nigh.

Enter DROMIO [OF] EPHESUS

ADRIANA   Say, is your tardy master now at hand?
DROMIO E.   Nay, he's at two hands with me, and that my two ears can   45
   witness.
ADRIANA   Say, didst thou speak with him? Know'st thou his mind?
DROMIO E.   Ay, ay, he told his mind upon mine ear.
   Beshrew his hand, I scarce could understand it.
LUCIANA   Spake he so doubtfully, thou couldst not feel his meaning?   50
DROMIO E.   Nay, he struck so plainly, I could too well feel his blows, and
   withal so doubtfully that I could scarce understand them.
ADRIANA   But say, I prithee, is he coming home?
   It seems he hath great care to please his wife.
DROMIO E.   Why, mistress, sure my master is horn-mad.   55
ADRIANA   Horn-mad, thou villain?
DROMIO E.   I mean not cuckold-mad,
   But sure he is stark mad.
   When I desired him to come home to dinner
   He asked me for a thousand marks in gold.
   ''Tis dinner-time', quoth I. 'My gold', quoth he.   60
   'Your meat doth burn', quoth I. 'My gold', quoth he.
   'Will you come home?' quoth I. 'My gold', quoth he.
   'Where is the thousand marks I gave thee, villain?'
   'The pig', quoth I, 'is burned.' 'My gold', quoth he.

45 two hands] F2; too hands F   48 Ay, ay,] I, I, F   59 thousand] F4 *(*1000 F2*)*; hundred F

40 **live . . . bereft** live to see yourself similarly
robbed of your rights (as a wife); or 'bereft' may,
as Onions suggests, mean 'impaired, spoilt'.
  41 This forbearance that marks you as a fool
will be abandoned. 'Fool-begged' is a coinage
apparently derived from the phrase 'to beg a person for a fool' (see Tilley F496) – referring to a
practice of petitioning in the Court of Wards for
custody of a lunatic (or a minor who was a Ward
of the Crown) in order to gain control of his
property.
  45 **at two hands** A reference to Dromio's
beating by Antipholus of Syracuse at 1.2.92–3;
possibly there is also a quibble on the phrase 'at
hands', with the sense of fighting at close quarters
(see *OED* Hand *sb* 25f).

48 **told** A quibble on 'tell' and 'toll'.
  49 **Beshrew** Curse, devil take (*OED*).
  49 **understand** Another quibble: 'understand'
and 'stand under'.
  50 **doubtfully** ambiguously.
  52 **doubtfully** dreadfully, frighteningly; as in
'doubtful' (1.1.68).
  55–6 **horn-mad** Dromio means 'furious', like
a horned beast attacking in rage. Adriana takes
him to refer to the horns of a cuckold.
  59 **thousand** F reads 'hundred', but this, as
NS notes, may be an error due to 'the use of
figures in the copy'; the context makes clear that
'thousand' is correct.

'My mistress, sir –' quoth I. 'Hang up thy mistress!   65
I know not thy mistress. Out on thy mistress!'

LUCIANA Quoth who?

DROMIO E. Quoth my master.
'I know', quoth he, 'no house, no wife, no mistress.'
So that my errand, due unto my tongue,   70
I thank him, I bare home upon my shoulders;
For, in conclusion, he did beat me there.

ADRIANA Go back again, thou slave, and fetch him home.

DROMIO E. Go back again and be new-beaten home?
For God's sake send some other messenger.   75

ADRIANA Back, slave, or I will break thy pate across.

DROMIO E. And he will bless that cross with other beating,
Between you I shall have a holy head.

ADRIANA Hence, prating peasant, fetch thy master home.
                    [*She beats Dromio*]

DROMIO E. Am I so round with you as you with me   80
That like a football you do spurn me thus?
You spurn me hence, and he will spurn me hither.
If I last in this service you must case me in leather.   [*Exit*]

LUCIANA Fie, how impatience loureth in your face.

ADRIANA His company must do his minions grace   85
Whilst I at home starve for a merry look.
Hath homely age th'alluring beauty took
From my poor cheek? Then he hath wasted it.
Are my discourses dull? barren my wit?
If voluble and sharp discourse be marred,   90

68–72] *As Pope; prose in* F   70 errand] F4; arrant F   83 SD *Exit*] F2; *not in* F

65 **hang up** to blazes with. Compare *Rom.* 3.3.57: 'Hang up philosophy!'

70 **my . . . tongue** the errand that I should have carried with my tongue. 'Upon my shoulders' (71) means 'in the form of a beating'. F's spelling 'arrant' is common.

77–8 Dromio suggests that two beatings will make the sign of the cross on his head. 'And' = if. 'Bless' quibbles on 'consecrate' and 'wound or hurt'; 'holy' on 'consecrated by a cross' and 'full of holes'.

79 **prating peasant** babbling rascal.

80 **round** outspoken; with a pun on the usual meaning, as the reference to football (81) makes clear; 'spurn' = kick, as in *1H6* 1.4.52: 'Spurn in pieces posts of adamant.' Dromio develops the image by saying that if he is to be kicked about he

ought to be cased in leather, like a football.

84 **loureth** scowls, or frowns.

85 **do . . . grace** give pleasure to his mistresses. Shakespeare often uses 'minion' (= darling) in this derogatory sense; compare 4.4.54.

86 **starve** Perhaps carries much of its original meaning of 'die'.

87 **homely age** Probably 'age which brings plainness'; this sense of 'homely' is not infrequent in Shakespeare.

88 **wasted** In both senses, as in *R2* 5.5.49: 'I wasted time, and now doth time waste me.'

89 **wit** powers of imagination or invention.

90 **voluble . . . discourse** fluent and witty conversation. The normal sense of 'sharp' is picked up in the image of a sharp instrument blunted by being struck against marble.

Unkindness blunts it more than marble hard.
Do their gay vestments his affections bait?
That's not my fault; he's master of my state.
What ruins are in me that can be found
By him not ruined? Then is he the ground   95
Of my defeatures. My decayèd fair
A sunny look of his would soon repair.
But, too unruly deer, he breaks the pale
And feeds from home. Poor I am but his stale.
LUCIANA   Self-harming jealousy! Fie, beat it hence.   100
ADRIANA   Unfeeling fools can with such wrongs dispense.
I know his eye doth homage otherwhere;
Or else what lets it but he would be here?
Sister, you know he promised me a chain.
Would that alone a love him would detain   105
So he would keep fair quarter with his bed.
I see the jewel best enamellèd
Will lose his beauty. Yet the gold bides still
That others touch; and often touching will
Wear gold, and no man that hath a name   110
But falsehood and corruption doth it shame.

105 alone a love him] *This edn, after Theobald;* alone, a loue he F   109–10 will / Wear] *Theobald;* will, / Where F
111 But] *Theobald;* By F

92 **his ... bait** tempt his feelings (of love);
'bait' = offer bait to.
93 **state** condition in life as reflected in her
appearance, clothes, etc. She herself has no 'gay
vestments' (92).
95 **ground** cause.
96 **defeatures** disfigurements; as at 5.1.300,
and *Venus and Adonis* 736.
96 **fair** fairness, beauty; a frequent usage in
Shakespeare.
98 **deer** With the common play on 'dear' (e.g.
Wiv. 5.5.118).
98 **pale** fence, paling.
99 **stale** tool; perhaps with the suggestion that
she is merely his harlot. Both senses are found in
Shakespeare (see Onions).
103 **lets ... here** prevents him from being
here.
105 Much disputed. F reads 'alone, a loue'; the
later Ff read 'alone, alone'. Foakes reads 'a toy',
arguing that in Secretary hand *t* might easily mistaken for *l*, and minim letters are notoriously
liable to confusion, so that 'toie' might well look
like 'loue'. Presumably the toy would be the chain
referred to in the preceding line. With Wells, I

prefer to keep the F 'a loue', tentatively suggesting
the emendation of 'he' to 'him'; it is tempting to
suppose that the compositor was disposed to set
up 'he would detain' by the parallel with 'he
would keep' in the following line. The two lines
would then mean, 'Would that only a love-affair
kept him from me, provided that he kept on good
terms with his (legitimate) wife.' This may be
awkward, but it is no more so than the alternatives
so far proposed. For 'kept on good terms', see
Onions.
107–11 Another difficult passage, almost
certainly corrupt, which none of the (usually
lengthy) explanations, embracing many emendations, has elucidated. I believe that the less
tampering with the text, the better, and that we
must content ourselves with a translation which
makes sense, even if it is not precisely what
Shakespeare intended. I accept Theobald's
emendation of F 'Where' to 'Wear' in 110, and of
'By' to 'But' in 111; I accept, too, the common
enough Elizabethan sense of 'jewel' (107) as any
'costly ornament, especially one made of gold,
silver, or precious stones' (*OED sb* 1); and I
translate: '[Even] the best-enamelled golden

> Since that my beauty cannot please his eye,
> I'll weep what's left away, and weeping die.
>
> LUCIANA How many fond fools serve mad jealousy!

Exeunt

2.2 *Enter* ANTIPHOLUS [OF SYRACUSE]

ANTIPHOLUS S. The gold I gave to Dromio is laid up
> Safe at the Centaur, and the heedful slave
> Is wandered forth in care to seek me out
> By computation and mine host's report.
> I could not speak with Dromio since at first   5
> I sent him from the mart. See, here he comes.

Enter DROMIO OF SYRACUSE

> How now, sir. Is your merry humour altered?
> As you love strokes, so jest with me again.
> You know no Centaur? You received no gold?
> Your mistress sent to have me home to dinner?   10
> My house was at the Phoenix? Wast thou mad
> That thus so madly thou didst answer me?

DROMIO S. What answer, sir? When spake I such a word?

ANTIPHOLUS S. Even now, even here, not half an hour since.

DROMIO S. I did not see you since you sent me hence   15
> Home to the Centaur with the gold you gave me.

Act 2, Scene 2   2.2] *Capell; not in* F   0 SD *Enter* ANTIPHOLUS OF SYRACUSE] *Enter Antipholis Errotis.* F   1 SH
ANTIPHOLUS S.] *Ant.* F *(thereafter / E. Ant., Ant., An., Anti., Antiph. / throughout scene)*   3–4 out / . . . report.] F; out. /
. . . report, *Rowe*   6 SD OF SYRACUSE] *Rowe;* Siracusia F   12 didst] F2; *did didst* F

ornament will lose its lustre; yet the gold itself
that people other than the owner handle remains
all the same; but frequent handling will wear away
[even] gold, and there is no man with a reputation
that is not soiled by falsehood and corruption.'
This version remains flawed, particularly in its
treatment of 'and' (110), but it makes reasonable
sense of a passage which apparently contains
unidentifiable compositorial misreadings.
   114 **fond** infatuated.

Act 2, Scene 2
   0 SD *Enter Antipholis Errotis.* is the F direction;
compare *Antipholis Erotes* in 1.2.0 SD. Having
verified that his gold is safe at the Centaur, Antipholus has returned to the market-place, where
he is joined by his own Dromio, whom he had

previously dispatched to the Centaur. He is close
to the house of his Ephesian twin from which
Adriana and Luciana emerge (100) and accost
him. The variations between blank verse, prose,
and couplets admirably reflect the changing
moods of the scene.
   2 **Centaur** See 1.2.9 and n.
   4 By reckoning where I am likely to be, and
according to what the host may be able to tell
him.
   14 ANTIPHOLUS S. F has *E.Ant.*, representing the ANTIPHOLUS ERROTIS of the opening
SD. This might be confusing, as the Dromios are
differentiated as *E. Dro.* and *S. Dro.*; but the context makes clear which Antipholus is intended.
For the remainder of the scene the SH for *Ant. S.*
is either *Ant.* or *An.* in F.

ANTIPHOLUS S. Villain, thou didst deny the gold's receipt,
    And told'st me of a mistress and a dinner,
    For which I hope thou felt'st I was displeased.
DROMIO S. I am glad to see you in this merry vein.   20
    What means this jest? I pray you, master, tell me.
ANTIPHOLUS S. Yea, dost thou jeer and flout me in the teeth?
    Think'st thou I jest? Hold, take thou that, and that.
                [He] beats Dromio
DROMIO S. Hold, sir, for God's sake; now your jest is earnest.
    Upon what bargain do you give it me?   25
ANTIPHOLUS S. Because that I familiarly sometimes
    Do use you for my fool, and chat with you,
    Your sauciness will jest upon my love,
    And make a common of my serious hours.
    When the sun shines let foolish gnats make sport,   30
    But creep in crannies when he hides his beams.
    If you will jest with me, know my aspect,
    And fashion your demeanour to my looks,
    Or I will beat this method in your sconce.
DROMIO S. 'Sconce' call you it? So you would leave battering I had rather   35
    have it a head. And you use these blows long I must get a sconce for
    my head, and ensconce it too, or else I shall seek my wit in my
    shoulders. But I pray, sir, why am I beaten?
ANTIPHOLUS S. Dost thou not know?
DROMIO S. Nothing, sir, but that I am beaten.   40
ANTIPHOLUS S. Shall I tell you why?
DROMIO S. Ay, sir, and wherefore; for they say every why hath a
    wherefore.

19 felt'st See 1.2.92, where the other Dromio felt Antipholus's displeasure in the form of a beating.

22 flout ... teeth insult me to my face; compare Tilley T429, 'To cast (hit) in the teeth'.

24 earnest Dromio puns on 'earnest' as a deposit laid down to secure a bargain.

28 jest upon trifle with.

29 And encroach on my serious hours as if they were common property.

30–1 The lines have a proverbial ring, but are not recorded as a proverb in Elizabethan times.

32 aspect In astrology the aspect of a planet was its position in relation to the other planets, and hence might exert a particular influence on human conduct. Dromio must adapt himself to the mood indicated by his master's looks. The stress falls on the second syllable of 'aspect'; compare 'aspects' (102).

34, 36 sconce Quibbles on 'sconce' = head (compare 1.2.79); 'sconce' = 'small fort or earthwork' (*OED* sv *sb.* 32 – compare 'so you would leave battering'); and 'sconce' = 'a protective screen' (*OED*) – compare 'I must get a sconce for my head'). 'Ensconce' embraces the last of these senses.

36–8 And ... shoulders i.e. if his head is too badly battered, his wit will have to retreat to his shoulders.

42–3 every ... wherefore Proverbial. See Tilley W331, 332.

ANTIPHOLUS S. Why, first for flouting me; and then wherefore –
    For urging it the second time to me.   45

DROMIO S. Was there ever any man thus beaten out of season,
    When in the why and the wherefore is neither rhyme nor reason?
    Well, sir, I thank you.

ANTIPHOLUS S.   Thank me, sir, for what?

DROMIO S. Marry, sir, for this something that you gave me for nothing.

ANTIPHOLUS S. I'll make you amends next, to give you nothing for   50
    something. But say, sir, is it dinner-time?

DROMIO S. No, sir. I think the meat wants that I have.

ANTIPHOLUS S. In good time, sir, what's that?

DROMIO Basting.

ANTIPHOLUS S. Well, sir, then 'twill be dry.   55

DROMIO S. If it be, sir, I pray you eat none of it.

ANTIPHOLUS S. Your reason?

DROMIO S. Lest it make you choleric, and purchase me another dry
    basting.

ANTIPHOLUS S. Well, sir, learn to jest in good time. There's a time for all   60
    things.

DROMIO S. I durst have denied that before you were so choleric.

ANTIPHOLUS S. By what rule, sir?

DROMIO S. Marry, sir, by a rule as plain as the plain bald pate of Father
    Time himself.   65

ANTIPHOLUS S. Let's hear it.

DROMIO S. There's no time for a man to recover his hair that grows bald
    by nature.

ANTIPHOLUS S. May he not do it by fine and recovery?

46–7] *As Capell; prose in* F   48–9] *As Rowe; prose in* F

46 out of season unseasonably, unfairly.

47 neither ... reason Proverbial. See Tilley
R98.

50–1 nothing for something nothing in
return for your services.

52 wants lacks.

53 In good time O indeed; a common
interjection.

54 Basting A pun on the culinary sense of the
word and the sense 'beating'.

58 choleric Of the four humours (see 1.2.21
n.) choler was credited with being hot and dry.
The balance of the humours could be affected by
what a man ate (see e.g. *Shr.* 4.1.170–2). The
choleric man was hot-tempered, or irritable.

58–9 dry basting severe drubbing; compare

'dry-beat' (*Rom.* 3.1.79).

60 in good time seasonably; however, as an
exclamation, as at 53 it means 'indeed'. 'There's a
time for all things' is proverbial. See Tilley T314.

64–5 Father Time Traditionally represented
as bald, except for a forelock. The jesting on
Time, and on baldness (see 77 n.), is carried on
to the end of the exchange (99).

69 fine and recovery As a legal term the
phrase refers to a process by which property not
normally transferable might be conveyed to
another person, and, in particular, a property
might be taken out of entail into full ownership.
The phrase picks up Dromio's 'recover' in the
previous line.

DROMIO S. Yes, to pay a fine for a periwig, and recover the lost hair of   70
another man.

ANTIPHOLUS S. Why is Time such a niggard of hair, being, as it is, so
plentiful an excrement?

DROMIO S. Because it is a blessing that he bestows on beasts, and what he
hath scanted men in hair he hath given them in wit.   75

ANTIPHOLUS S. Why, but there's many a man hath more hair than wit.

DROMIO S. Not a man of those but he hath the wit to lose his hair.

ANTIPHOLUS S. Why, thou didst conclude hairy men plain dealers,
without wit.

DROMIO S. The plainer dealer, the sooner lost; yet he loseth it in a kind of   80
jollity.

ANTIPHOLUS S. For what reason?

DROMIO S. For two, and sound ones too.

ANTIPHOLUS S. Nay, not sound, I pray you.

DROMIO S. Sure ones, then.   85

ANTIPHOLUS S. Nay, not sure in a thing falsing.

DROMIO S. Certain ones, then.

ANTIPHOLUS S. Name them.

DROMIO S. The one, to save the money that he spends in tiring; the
other, that at dinner they should not drop in his porridge.   90

ANTIPHOLUS S. You would all this time have proved there is no time for
all things.

DROMIO S. Marry, and did, sir; namely, e'en no time to recover hair lost
by nature.

ANTIPHOLUS S. But your reason was not substantial, why there is no   95
time to recover.

75 men] *Theobald;* them F   89 tiring] *Pope;* trying F   93 e'en] *Malone, conj. Capell;* in F; *omitted later* Ff

70 **fine** fee (for a wig made of human hair).
Foakes reminds us that 'Hair was bought and
sold to make wigs', comparing *MV* 3.2.88 ff.

73 **excrement** This could denote any out-
growth of the human body (*OED* sv *sb²*); compare
LLL 5.1.103: 'dally with my excrement, with my
mustachio'. In this general sense it is obsolete.

75 **scanted** been niggardly to.

75 **men** F reads 'them'. The context corrobor-
ates Theobald's emendation.

75 **wit** intelligence.

76 **there's . . . wit** Proverbial. See Tilley B736,
and compare *TGV* 3.1.353, 358: 'she hath more
hair than wit'.

77 **the wit . . . hair** Probably, as Dr Johnson
notes, an allusion to one of the consequences of
syphilis; compare *MND* 1.2.97.

78 **plain dealers** straightforward men, men
without deceit; the following lines suggest that
the pun with 'men who deal with women' has
already begun.

80–1 Dromio interprets plain dealing as direct-
ness in their dealings with women, so that they
very soon lose their hair in jolly (i.e. sexual)
encounters.

83, 84 **sound** A quibble on two senses of
'sound': 'valid' and 'healthy'.

86 **falsing** deceptive.

89 **tiring** dressing his hair; 'they' refers to his
hairs.

90 **porridge** soup; the implication of hair
dropping out as a result of venereal disease is
continued.

DROMIO S. Thus I mend it: Time himself is bald, and therefore to the
world's end will have bald followers.
ANTIPHOLUS S. I knew 'twould be a bald conclusion. But soft, who wafts
us yonder?   100

                   Enter ADRIANA *and* LUCIANA

ADRIANA Ay, ay, Antipholus, look strange and frown;
           Some other mistress hath thy sweet aspects.
           I am not Adriana, nor thy wife.
           The time was once when thou unurged wouldst vow
           That never words were music to thine ear,   105
           That never object pleasing in thine eye,
           That never touch well welcome to thy hand,
           That never meat sweet-savoured in thy taste,
           Unless I spake, or looked, or touched, or carved to thee.
           How comes it now, my husband, O, how comes it,   110
           That thou art then estrangèd from thyself?
           Thyself I call it, being strange to me
           That undividable, incorporate,
           Am better than thy dear self's better part.
           Ah, do not tear away thyself from me;   115
           For know, my love, as easy mayst thou fall
           A drop of water in the breaking gulf,
           And take unmingled thence that drop again
           Without addition or diminishing,
           As take from me thyself, and not me too.   120
           How dearly would it touch thee to the quick
           Shouldst thou but hear I were licentious,

99 bald conclusion trivial conclusion; this
rounds off the puns on baldness.
99 wafts beckons.
101–37 This passage, with its lyrical references
to the delights of early love, is the most eloquent
account in the play of the marriage bond, when
man and wife are one flesh, 'undividable,
incorporate'. At the same time there is the absurd
circumstance that Adriana is talking to the twin
image of her other half.
101 look strange look as though we were
strangers.
102 aspects looks; compare 32.
105–11 The re-echoing words 'That never
. . .', leading to a climax in 111, are an example of
the rhetorical figure *anaphora*, here expressing
Adriana's recollection of the early days of her
intimacy with her husband.

114 better part better qualities, or soul.
Adriana plays poignantly on the idea that Antipholus is estranged from himself, from her, and
from his own better nature. The audience is of
course aware that the Antipholus she is addressing is another division of the self.
116–17 Compare the proverb (Tilley D613),
'As lost as a drop of water in the sea'. We recall
Antipholus of Syracuse's use of this image
(1.2.35–8) to signify his feeling that he has lost
his identity.
116 fall let fall.
121 dearly intensely; compare *Ham.* 4.3.41:
'as we dearly grieve'.
121 touch ... quick Proverbial; see Tilley
Q13: 'He touches him to the Quick.'

And that this body, consecrate to thee,
By ruffian lust should be contaminate?
Wouldst thou not spit at me, and spurn at me,   125
And hurl the name of husband in my face,
And tear the stained skin off my harlot brow,
And from my false hand cut the wedding ring,
And break it with a deep-divorcing vow?
I know thou canst, and therefore see thou do it.   130
I am possessed with an adulterate blot.
My blood is mingled with the crime of lust;
For if we two be one, and thou play false,
I do digest the poison of thy flesh,
Being strumpeted by thy contagion.   135
Keep then fair league and truce with thy true bed,
I live unstained, thou undishonourèd.

ANTIPHOLUS S. Plead you to me, fair dame? I know you not.
In Ephesus I am but two hours old,
As strange unto your town as to your talk,   140
Who, every word by all my wit being scanned,
Wants wit in all one word to understand.

LUCIANA Fie, brother, how the world is changed with you.
When were you wont to use my sister thus?
She sent for you by Dromio home to dinner.   145

ANTIPHOLUS S. By Dromio?

DROMIO S. By me?

ADRIANA By thee; and this thou didst return from him,
That he did buffet thee, and in his blows

---

127 off] *Hanmer;* of F   132 crime] F; grime *Warburton*   137 unstained] *Hanmer, conj. Theobald;* distain'd F; dis-stain'd *Theobald;* undistain'd *Keightley*   147 me?] *Rowe;* me F

127 Editors note the similarity between this and Laertes' 'brands the harlot / Even here, between the chaste unsmirched brow / Of my true mother' (*Ham.* 4.5.119). The brow proverbially (Tilley F590) gave indication of character. Wells thinks there may also be an allusion to the punishment of branding.

131 **blot** stain, disgrace.

132 **crime** Warburton, followed by some recent editors (e.g. NS), emended this to 'grime', linking it with 'blot' in the previous line and 'unstained' (F 'distain'd') in 137. The change seems unnecessary.

133 **we . . . one** See 101–37 n.

135 **strumpeted . . . contagion** turned into a whore by contamination from you.

136 **Keep** If you keep.

137 **unstained** The F 'distain'd' has been much discussed. The word is found elsewhere in Shakespeare with the sense of 'sullied' or 'dishonoured', which will not do here. Foakes suggests that here it 'could easily have arisen as a compositor's error by attraction from "undishonour'd"'. Emendations that have been suggested, with varying degrees of plausibility, are 'dis-stain'd' and 'undistain'd'. On grounds both of sense and of metre, I follow the 'unstained' of Hanmer and of most modern editors.

141 **Who** And I. However, as though it were in the third person, it is followed by 'wants'.

Denied my house for his, me for his wife.   150
ANTIPHOLUS S. Did you converse, sir, with this gentlewoman?
    What is the course and drift of your compact?
DROMIO S. I, sir? I never saw her till this time.
ANTIPHOLUS S. Villain, thou liest, for even her very words
    Didst thou deliver to me on the mart.   155
DROMIO S. I never spake with her in all my life.
ANTIPHOLUS S. How can she thus then call us by our names –
    Unless it be by inspiration?
ADRIANA How ill agrees it with your gravity
    To counterfeit thus grossly with your slave,   160
    Abetting him to thwart me in my mood.
    Be it my wrong, you are from me exempt;
    But wrong not that wrong with a more contempt.
    Come, I will fasten on this sleeve of thine.
    Thou art an elm, my husband, I a vine,   165
    Whose weakness, married to thy stronger state,
    Makes me with thy strength to communicate.
    If aught possess thee from me, it is dross,
    Usurping ivy, briar, or idle moss,
    Who, all for want of pruning, with intrusion   170
    Infect thy sap, and live on thy confusion.
ANTIPHOLUS S. [*Aside*] To me she speaks; she moves me for her theme.
    What, was I married to her in my dream?
    Or sleep I now, and think I hear all this?

157–8 names – / . . . inspiration?] *This edn;* names? / . . . inspiration. F   166 stronger] F3; stranger F

152 **course . . . compact** gist and scope of
your collusion (with her).
   155 **mart** This suggests that Antipholus and
Dromio have moved across the stage (the whole
of which represents the open space of the
market-place – see nn. on location for 1.1 and for
the present scene) to a spot near the Phoenix,
whence Adriana and Luciana have issued.
   162–3 Let us accept that it is my fault that you
are alienated from me, but do not make that fault
more grievous by treating it with greater con-
tempt. The transition to couplets marks Adriana's
softened mood and, perhaps, Antipholus's
acceptance of a perplexing situation.
   165 **elm . . . vine** In ancient times vines were
often trained on elms; compare the proverb, 'the
vine embraces the elm' (Tilley v61). There is a
close parallel in a passage referring to marriage in
Ovid, *Metamorphoses* 14.665–6, and an allusion to
a wife as a fruitful vine in Ps. 128.3. We may note

the contrast (and resemblance) between the fruitful vine clinging to the elm and the 'usurping ivy'
(169) infecting the sap.
   167 **with . . . communicate** share in your
strength.
   168 If anything, apart from me, takes possession of you, it is rubbish. 'Possess' has a stronger
meaning than that of today; here, as in 131, it is
almost akin to 'infect' (171).
   169 **idle** useless.
   170–1 **Who . . . confusion** Which, entirely for
lack of curbing, poisons your essential self, and
lives by destroying you. 'Intrusion' suggests
forced entry. 'Confusion', as normally in
Shakespeare, implies 'destruction'.
   172–7 Foakes compares the feelings of
Sebastian in *TN* 4.1, when, 'addressed by Olivia
as if he were almost her husband, he accepts what
is to him a fantastic situation . . ., "If it be thus to
dream, still let me sleep."'

What error drives our eyes and ears amiss?   175
Until I know this sure uncertainty,
I'll entertain the offered fallacy.

LUCIANA Dromio, go bid the servants spread for dinner.

DROMIO S. [*Aside*] O for my beads! I cross me for a sinner.
This is the fairy land. O spite of spites,   180
We talk with goblins, owls, and sprites;
If we obey them not, this will ensue:
They'll suck our breath, or pinch us black and blue.

LUCIANA Why prat'st thou to thyself, and answer'st not?
Dromio, thou Dromio, thou snail, thou slug, thou sot.   185

DROMIO S. I am transformèd, master, am not I?

ANTIPHOLUS S. I think thou art in mind, and so am I.

DROMIO S. Nay, master, both in mind and in my shape.

ANTIPHOLUS S. Thou hast thine own form.

DROMIO S.   No, I am an ape.

LUCIANA If thou art changed to aught, 'tis to an ass.   190

DROMIO S. 'Tis true, she rides me, and I long for grass.
'Tis so, I am an ass, else it could never be
But I should know her as well as she knows me.

177 the offered] *Capell* (offer'd); the free'd F   181 goblins, owls, and sprites] F; Goblins, Owles and Elves and
Sprights F2; goblins, owls and elvish sprites *Pope*; goblins, ouphs and sprites *Theobald*; fairies, goblins, elves and sprites
Cuningham   185 thou Dromio] F; thou drone *Theobald*; thou drumble *Riverside*   186 not I] *Theobald*; I not F

175 error It is one of the leading errors of the
comedy.

176 know ... uncertainty can understand
what is certainly a mystery.

177 entertain ... fallacy accept the delusion
with which I am faced.

177 the offered F reads 'the free'd'. NS suggests that this probably resulted from a compositorial misreading of MS. *thofred* or *the ofred*.
In Secretary hand *o* and *e* are not always easily
distinguished.

179 beads ... sinner This seems not amiss in
a play which owes so much to Christian allusion.

181 Need we be worried by a line which is
metrically short? It is effective. Various sugges-
tions have been made to regularise the line, but
none has authority. Many editors, including
Foakes, emend 'owls' to 'elves', but Foakes
observes, on the authority of J. Baret's *Dictionary*
(1580), that screech-owls might have dealings
with children, and he is not convincing in justify-
ing his emendation 'elves' on the grounds that
'the compositor saw *olwes* in the MS., ... and
made sense of it by transposing letters'.
Theobald's 'ouphs' (preferred by Philip Brock-

bank) gives another spirit in human form (see
Wiv. 4.4.50) and could also be misread as *owls*.

183 breath breath of life.

183 pinch ... blue Pinching was a traditional
punishment associated with fairies; the idea is
often found in Shakespeare, as, e.g., the punishment ordained for Falstaff in *Wiv.* To pinch black
and blue was proverbial; see Tilley B160.

185 Dromio, thou Dromio The F reading.
Most editors have followed Theobald's emendation, 'Dromio, thou drone', as being metrically
smoother, palaeographically plausible, and in
tune with the rest of the line; but none of these
reasons is in itself persuasive enough to justify the
change if we accept that Luciana is addressing
Dromio generically as the type of lazy, idiotic
('sot') slave, as at 3.1.10 Dromio of Ephesus is
addressed as the generic drunkard.

186–90 Transformation is a central theme of
the play.

189 ape By 'ape' Dromio suggests (a) something counterfeit, as in *Cym.* 2.2.31, 'O sleep,
thou ape of death', and (b) a dupe, or fool (as in
Rom. 2.1.16), which Luciana picks up in saying
that he is changed to an ass.

ADRIANA Come, come, no longer will I be a fool,
    To put the finger in the eye and weep   195
    Whilst man and master laughs my woes to scorn.
    Come, sir, to dinner. Dromio, keep the gate.
    Husband, I'll dine above with you today,
    And shrive you of a thousand idle pranks.
    Sirrah, if any ask you for your master,   200
    Say he dines forth, and let no creature enter.
    Come, sister. Dromio, play the porter well.
ANTIPHOLUS S. [*Aside*] Am I in earth, in heaven, or in hell?
    Sleeping or waking? mad or well advised?
    Known unto these, and to myself disguised?   205
    I'll say as they say, and persever so,
    And in this mist at all adventures go.
DROMIO S. Master, shall I be porter at the gate?
ADRIANA Ay, and let none enter, lest I break your pate.
LUCIANA Come, come, Antipholus, we dine too late.   210

                                               [*Exeunt*]

3.1 *Enter* ANTIPHOLUS OF EPHESUS, *his man* DROMIO, ANGELO *the*
goldsmith, and BALTHASAR *the merchant*

ANTIPHOLUS E. Good Signior Angelo, you must excuse us all.
    My wife is shrewish when I keep not hours.

204–5 waking? . . . advised? / . . . disguised?] *This edn;* waking, . . . advisde: / . . . disguisde: F   **210** SD *Exeunt*] *Rowe;*
not in F   **Act 3, Scene 1   3.1**] *Actus Tertius. Scena Prima.* F   **0** SD] *As in* F   **1** SH ANTIPHOLUS E.] *E. Anti.* F
(thereafter / E. Ant., Anti., Ant. / throughout scene)

195 To act childishly or foolishly; compare
Tilley F229: 'to put Finger in the eye'.
197–209 Dromio . . . pate We are prepared
for the events of the coming scene. Is there a hint
of hell-gate, with Dromio as devil–porter?
199 shrive you of hear your confession and
grant you forgiveness for.
201 forth away from home.
204 well advised in my right mind.
206 persever Normally accented on the
second syllable in Shakespeare.
207 mist confusion.
207 at all adventures whatever the risks or
consequences.

Act 3, Scene 1
  0 SD As in F.
  1 SH ANTIPHOLUS E. *E. Anti.* in F. From now

on the confusions between the two Antipholuses
(together with their slaves) are in a sense the main
action of the play. The F speech headings
(variously *E. Anti., E. An., E. Ant., Anti., Ant., S.*
Anti.) do not always distinguish the two; in this
edition they are distinguished as ANTIPHOLUS
E. and ANTIPHOLUS S. The scene clearly takes
place at the door of Antipholus of Ephesus's
house, and his entry (at last) causes new confusions. The loose rhymed couplets (11–85), in
lines of varying length, are appropriate to the
comedy of the situation. The blank verse at the
end of the scene marks a return to common
sense.
  2 keep not hours am unpunctual.

Say that I lingered with you at your shop
To see the making of her carcanet,
And that tomorrow you will bring it home.   5
But here's a villain that would face me down
He met me on the mart, and that I beat him,
And charged him with a thousand marks in gold,
And that I did deny my wife and house.
Thou drunkard, thou, what didst thou mean by this?   10

DROMIO E. Say what you will, sir, but I know what I know:
That you beat me at the mart I have your hand to show.
If the skin were parchment and the blows you gave were ink,
Your own handwriting would tell you what I think.

ANTIPHOLUS E. I think thou art an ass.

DROMIO E.   Marry, so it doth appear   15
By the wrongs I suffer, and the blows I bear.
I should kick, being kicked, and, being at that pass,
You would keep from my heels, and beware of an ass.

ANTIPHOLUS E. You're sad, Signior Balthasar. Pray God our cheer
May answer my good will, and your good welcome here.   20

BALTHASAR I hold your dainties cheap, sir, and your welcome dear.

ANTIPHOLUS E. O, Signior Balthasar, either at flesh or fish·
A table full of welcome makes scarce one dainty dish.

BALTHASAR Good meat, sir, is common. That every churl affords.

ANTIPHOLUS E. And welcome more common, for that's nothing but   25
words.

BALTHASAR Small cheer and great welcome makes a merry feast.

24 common. That] *This edn, after Theobald* (common; that)*;* common that F

4 **carcanet** jewelled necklace – i.e. the 'chain' referred to at 2.1.104 and at 115 in the present scene.

6 **face me down** outface me, impudently insist.

8 **charged** entrusted.

9 **deny** disown.

11–85 This long passage of couplets, in which the lines vary from four to seven stresses, lends zest and tempo to what is potentially a bitter exchange.

11 **I . . . know** Proverbial, amply illustrated in Tilley K173.

15, 18 **ass** Compare 2.2.190, in which the other Dromio is labelled an ass; this is in key with the important theme of transformation.

17 **at that pass** in such a predicament.

19–29 As Foakes observes, 'This debate on the relative importance of good welcome and good cheer is carried on in commonplaces . . . and cast in rhyme; it is not . . . a serious debate, but a trial of courtesy, recalling . . . the custom of discussing a set theme at a supper or social gathering.' As parallels Foakes cites Castiglione, *The Courtier*, trans. Hoby (1561), Tudor Translations, 1900, pp. 33 ff., and Lyly, *Euphues and his England* (1580), ed. Bond, 1902, II, 161–2, where this topic is canvassed.

19 **sad** serious.

19 **cheer** fare, entertainment.

23 The warmest welcome is not equivalent to even a single good dish.

ANTIPHOLUS E. Ay, to a niggardly host and more sparing guest.
      But though my cates be mean, take them in good part.
      Better cheer may you have, but not with better heart.
      But soft, my door is locked. Go bid them let us in.   30
DROMIO E. Maud, Bridget, Marian, Cicely, Gillian, Ginn!
DROMIO S. [*Within*] Mome, malthorse, capon, coxcomb, idiot, patch,
      Either get thee from the door or sit down at the hatch.
      Dost thou conjure for wenches, that thou callest for such store,
      When one is one too many? Go, get thee from the door.   35
DROMIO E. What patch is made our porter? My master stays in the
      street.
DROMIO S. [*Within*] Let him walk from whence he came, lest he catch
      cold on's feet.
ANTIPHOLUS E. Who talks within, there? Ho, open the door.
DROMIO S. [*Within*] Right, sir, I'll tell you when and you'll tell me
      wherefore.
ANTIPHOLUS E. Wherefore? For my dinner. I have not dined today.   40
DROMIO S. [*Within*] Nor today here you must not. Come again when
      you may.
ANTIPHOLUS E. What art thou that keepest me out from the house I
      owe?
DROMIO S. [*Within*] The porter for this time, sir, and my name is
      Dromio.
DROMIO E. O, villain, thou hast stolen both mine office and my name.

32 SD *Within*] *Rowe (throughout scene); not in* F   41 not. Come] not; come F4; *not* come F

28 **cates** provisions
31 The roll-call of six serving-wenches gives a notion of Antipholus's wealth and standing.
32 SD Here, and on the ten subsequent occasions on which Dromio S., inside the house, mocks or abuses the group outside, F gives no SD. But how is Dromio to be clearly heard, perhaps seen, by the audience? At 47 F gives the SD *Enter Luce*, and at 60 *Enter Adriana*; clearly both must be visible to the audience, and so at both places I add '[*above*]'. For possible ways of staging this episode see pp. 23–5 above.
32 Admirably picks up the rhythm of the previous line, and thus adds force to Dromio E.'s insulting riposte: 'Blockhead, stupid drudge [like a brewer's horse], eunuch ['capon'], fool [the 'fools' employed to amuse noble or courtly households often wore cocks' combs], idiot, and again fool [the 'fools' often wore 'patched' or pied garments]'.

33 Either go away from the door, or be silent. A modern Dromio might have said, more coarsely, 'Either clear out or shut up.' Tilley, under 'It is good to have a Hatch within the door' (H207), gives many examples, though not the present one, of similar phrases used in the sense of 'keep silent'. Compare *OED* Hatch *sb* 1b: figurative, 'esp. in proverbial phrase, *To keep (set, have) a hatch before the door*: to keep silence. *Obs.*' *OED* gives four examples between 1555 and 1594, but again not Dromio's use of the expression.
34 **conjure for** bring into being by magic incantations.
37 **catch ... feet** Not, I think, used, as Wells suggests, in the sense of the 'Lombard proverb' cited by Jonson (*Volpone* 2.2.40), meaning 'to have to sell cheap'; Dromio S. is merely being derisive.
39 **I'll ... wherefore** Akin to the proverb noted at 2.2.42–3; 'and' = if.
42 **owe** own.

The one ne'er got me credit, the other mickle blame.   45
If thou hadst been Dromio today in my place,
Thou wouldst have changed thy face for a name, or thy name
    for an ass.

Enter LUCE [*above*]

LUCE What a coil is there, Dromio! Who are those at the gate?

DROMIO E. Let my master in, Luce.

LUCE   Faith, no, he comes too late,
    And so tell your master.

DROMIO E.   O lord, I must laugh.   50
    Have at you with a proverb: 'Shall I set in my staff?'

LUCE Have at you with another. That's 'When? Can you tell?'

DROMIO S. [*Within*] If thy name be called Luce, Luce, thou hast
    answered him well.

ANTIPHOLUS E. Do you hear, you minion? You'll let us in, I trow.

LUCE I thought to have asked you.

DROMIO S. [*Within*]   And you said no.   55

DROMIO E. So come – help. Well struck! There was blow for blow.

ANTIPHOLUS E. Thou baggage, let me in.

LUCE   Can you tell for whose sake?

DROMIO E. Master, knock the door hard.

LUCE   Let him knock till it ache.

ANTIPHOLUS E. You'll cry for this, minion, if I beat the door down.

47] *As* F; *thy office* (*for thy face*) *Foakes;* an aim (*for a name*) NS; a face (*for an ass*) *Collier*   47 SD *Enter* LUCE *above*] *Enter Luce* F; *Luce within* / *Rowe; Luce, the kitchen-maid, comes out upon the balcony* / NS, *conj. Dyce;* LUCE] *concealed from Antipholus of Ephesus and his companions*] / *Foakes*   49–51] *As Rowe;* late, . . . Master. / O . . . laugh . . . Proverbe, / . . . staffe F   54 trow] *Theobald;* hope F

45 credit ... blame Wells notes: 'It is his *name* that might have got him *credit*, his *office* (or duties) that has got him *blame*.'

47 Even in a passage which is metrically so unusual, with a varying number of stresses in the lines, this line is very inept, and the apparent impossibility of finding sense in it confirms that it is corrupt. Of the emendations proposed, among the more helpful is NS, 'an aim' for 'a name', in the sense of 'butt' or 'mark'; this would relate the line more clearly to Dromio's having been made a butt by being called an ass (15–18), but adds little clarification. Accepting this change, Foakes goes further, and emends 'thy face' to 'thy office'. In perplexity, I leave the line as it stands in F.

48 coil commotion.

51 set ... staff set myself up here [outside the house]; compare Tilley T804.

52 When? ... tell? An expression of defiance; perhaps 'Just as you like'; see Tilley T88.

53 Luce, Luce Is there perhaps a play on the name – 'loose'?

54 minion hussy, minx.

54 trow trust, suppose. Theobald's emendation of F 'hope' to 'trow' is hard to justify, except for the sake of the rhyme, and for this I accept it. Since there are other triple rhymes in the exchange, Malone's suggestion that a line may have dropped out can be disregarded.

55 I thought ... you Spoken derisively.

56 Dromio and his master are apparently hammering the door alternately, striking physical blows in response to the verbal blows from within.

LUCE What needs all that, and a pair of stocks in the town?   60

Enter ADRIANA [*above*]

ADRIANA Who is that at the door that keeps all this noise?
DROMIO S. [*Within*] By my troth, your town is troubled with unruly
　　boys.
ANTIPHOLUS E. Are you there, wife? You might have come before.
ADRIANA Your wife, sir knave? Go get you from the door.
　　　　　　　　　　　　　　　　　　　　　　　[*Exit with Luce*]
DROMIO E. If you went in pain, master, this knave would go sore.   65
ANGELO Here is neither cheer, sir, nor welcome. We would fain have
　　either.
BALTHASAR In debating which was best, we shall part with neither.
DROMIO E. They stand at the door, master. Bid them welcome hither.
ANTIPHOLUS E. There is something in the wind, that we cannot get in.
DROMIO E. You would say so, master, if your garments were thin.   70
　　Your cake is warm within. You stand here in the cold.
　　It would make a man mad as a buck to be so bought and sold.
ANTIPHOLUS E. Go fetch me something. I'll break ope the gate.
DROMIO S. [*Within*] Break any breaking here, and I'll break your
　　knave's pate.
DROMIO E. A man may break a word with you, sir, and words are but
　　wind;   75
　　Ay, and break it in your face, so he break it not behind.
DROMIO S. [*Within*] It seems thou wantest breaking. Out upon thee,
　　hind!
DROMIO E. Here's too much 'Out upon thee.' I pray thee, let me in.

60 SD *Enter* ADRIANA *above*] Enter Adriana F; *within* / Rowe; to Luce / Foakes   64 SD *Exit with Luce*] NS (subst.)   71
cake] cake here F   75 you, sir] F2; your sir F

60 **and a pair** since there is a pair, or set.
65 **If you were to go** in pain (beaten, or put in
the stocks), it would go hard with me (myself,
actually a knave, your servant).
66 **cheer ... welcome** See 19–29, where
Antipholus E. promises Angelo and Balthasar
good cheer and welcome at his house.
67 **part** depart.
68 **Bid them welcome** Ironical.
69 **something in the wind** something wrong.
Dromio in his retort (70) treats the phrase
literally as if a cold wind were actually blowing.
71 **cake ... warm** Presumably refers to
Adriana, who is warm indoors, a good meal

before her, and her (supposed) husband with her;
'cake' possibly also referring to woman as a dainty
morsel; compare *Tro.* 1.1.15–24. In the F reading
'cake here' the 'here' is obtrusive – probably an
anticipation of the 'here' later in the line.
72 **mad as a buck** Proverbial for anger; see
Tilley B697. Foakes suggests that it may be
related to 'horn-mad' (2.1.55).
75 **break a word** speak; coarsely punned on in
the following line.
75 **words ... wind** Proverbial.
77 **thou wantest breaking** you need to be
broken in by a thrashing.
77 **hind** boorish fellow.

DROMIO S. [*Within*] Ay, when fowls have no feathers, and fish have no
      fin.
ANTIPHOLUS E. Well, I'll break in. Go borrow me a crow.   80
DROMIO E. A crow without feather, master? Mean you so?
      For a fish without a fin, there's a fowl without a feather.
      If a crow help us in, sirrah, we'll pluck a crow together.
ANTIPHOLUS E. Go, get thee gone. Fetch me an iron crow.
BALTHASAR Have patience, sir. O, let it not be so.   85
      Herein you war against your reputation,
      And draw within the compass of suspect
      Th'unviolated honour of your wife.
      Once this: your long experience of her wisdom,
      Her sober virtue, years, and modesty,   90
      Plead on her part some cause to you unknown.
      And doubt not, sir, but she will well excuse
      Why at this time the doors are made against you.
      Be ruled by me. Depart in patience,
      And let us to the Tiger all to dinner,   95
      And about evening come yourself alone
      To know the reason of this strange restraint.
      If by strong hand you offer to break in
      Now in the stirring passage of the day,
      A vulgar comment will be made of it,   100
      And that supposèd by the common rout
      Against your yet ungallèd estimation
      That may with foul intrusion enter in
      And dwell upon your grave when you are dead.
      For slander lives upon succession,   105
      For ever housèd where it gets possession.
ANTIPHOLUS E. You have prevailed. I will depart in quiet,

81 Mean you so?] F4; mean you so; F   89 her] *Pope;* your F

79 Perhaps proverbial, but not so recorded. A reference in Warner's translation of the *Menaechmi* to 'birdes that beare feathers, or fishes that have finnes' is discussed at p. 9 above.

83 **pluck a crow** Proverbial for settling a quarrel; see Tilley C855.

85, 94 **patience** We recall Luciana's admonition to Adriana to 'be patient' (2.1.9) and Adriana's brushing aside of the advice (32, 41). Husband and wife alike seem given to impatience.

87 **suspect** suspicion.

89 **Once this** In short, to sum up.

92 **excuse** explain.

95 **Tiger** Presumably an inn.

99 **stirring passage** bustling traffic.

100 **vulgar** public.

102 **ungallèd estimation** unsullied reputation.

103 **intrusion** forceful breaking in; compare 2.2.170.

105 **lives upon succession** passes on from generation to generation.

And in despite of mirth mean to be merry.
I know a wench of excellent discourse,
Pretty and witty; wild, and yet, too, gentle.   110
There will we dine. This woman that I mean,
My wife (but, I protest, without desert)
Hath oftentimes upbraided me withal.
To her will we to dinner. [*To Angelo*] Get you home
And fetch the chain. By this, I know, 'tis made.   115
Bring it, I pray you, to the Porpentine,
For there's the house. That chain will I bestow –
Be it for nothing but to spite my wife –
Upon mine hostess there. Good sir, make haste.
Since mine own doors refuse to entertain me,   120
I'll knock elsewhere to see if they'll disdain me.
ANGELO I'll meet you at that place some hour hence.
ANTIPHOLUS E. Do so. – This jest shall cost me some expense.

Exeunt

3.2 *Enter* LUCIANA, *with* ANTIPHOLUS OF SYRACUSE

LUCIANA And may it be that you have quite forgot
          A husband's office? Shall, Antipholus,
          Even in the spring of love thy love-springs rot?
          Shall love in building grow so ruinous?

---

110 yet, too, gentle] *Rowe;* yet too gentle F   114 *To Angelo*] *Cam.; not in* F   **Act 3, Scene 2   3.2** *Pope; not in* F   0 SD]
Enter Iuliana, with Antipholus of Siracusia F   1 SH LUCIANA] *Iulia.* F   4 building] *Theobald;* buildings F   4 ruinous]
Capell, conj. Theobald; ruinate F

108 **in despite . . . merry** in spite of mockery
intend to be merry.
110 **wild** Probably means no more than 'lively'.
110 **gentle** Probably intended to carry the normal sense 'well-bred', combined perhaps with the
modern sense of the word.
115 **chain** i.e. the carcanet referred to at 4,
called a 'chain' by Adriana (2.1.104).
116 **Porpentine** The Courtesan's house; the
normal form for 'porcupine' in Shakespeare.

Act 3, Scene 2

0 SD, 1 SH LUCIANA For the stage direction F
reads *Iuliana,* and for the first speech heading
Iulia. Clearly Luciana is intended, and the mistake is not satisfactorily accounted for – unless
Err. was close in composition to *TGV,* and
Shakespeare for the moment had that play in
mind. Presumably Luciana and Antipholus make
their entry from the house which is the location of

the preceding scene. The language and versification are discussed at pp. 19–20 above; together
with the subject-matter (marital relations) of the
first 70 lines, they have much in common with the
exchange between Luciana and Adriana in 2.1.
3 **love-springs** tender springs of love;
'springs' is used in the sense of young shoots of
trees; compare *OED* Spring *sb*[1] 9.
4 **building** The accepted emendation of F
'buildings'. For the image compare *TGV* 5.4.10,
and *Tro.* 4.2.103: 'the strong base and building of
my love'.
4 **ruinous** The 'ruinate' of F is normally
emended to 'ruinous', partly to preserve the
rhyme, partly because 'ruinate' is used only as a
verb on the three other occasions when it appears
in Shakespeare (see *Harvard Concordance*); compare 'ruinous' in the passage from *TGV* cited
above.

If you did wed my sister for her wealth,   5
   Then for her wealth's sake use her with more kindness;
Or if you like elsewhere, do it by stealth.
   Muffle your false love with some show of blindness;
Let not my sister read it in your eye.
   Be not thy tongue thy own shame's orator.   10
Look sweet, speak fair, become disloyalty;
   Apparel vice like virtue's harbinger.
Bear a fair presence, though your heart be tainted;
   Teach sin the carriage of a holy saint.
Be secret-false; what need she be acquainted? –   15
   What simple thief brags of his own attaint?
'Tis double wrong to truant with your bed
   And let her read it in thy looks at board.
Shame hath a bastard fame, well managèd;
   Ill deeds is doubled with an evil word.   20
Alas, poor women, make us but believe,
   Being compact of credit, that you love us.
Though others have the arm, show us the sleeve.
   We in your motion turn, and you may move us.
Then, gentle brother, get you in again.   25
   Comfort my sister, cheer her, call her wife.
'Tis holy sport to be a little vain
   When the sweet breath of flattery conquers strife.
ANTIPHOLUS S. Sweet mistress, what your name is else I know not,
   Nor by what wonder you do hit of mine.   30
Less in your knowledge and your grace you show not
   Than our earth's wonder, more than earth divine.

16 attaint] *Rowe;* attaine F   20 is] F; are F2   21 but] *Pope;* not F   26 wife] F2; wise F

8 Conceal your false love by blindfolding (yourself and my sister).

10 **orator** spokesman.

11 **become disloyalty** let your infidelity be displayed with a fair outward show.

12 Make your vice look like a fore-runner of virtue; compare Tilley v44: 'Vice is often clothed in virtue's habit.'

14 **carriage** bearing, mien; compare Tilley T140: 'Fair face, foul heart'.

16 **attaint** disgrace, corruption.

17 **truant ... bed** be unfaithful to your wife. Luciana assumes too much.

18 **at board** at table.

19 **bastard fame** illegitimate honour.

20 Proverbial; see Tilley w800: 'Fine words dress ill deeds.'

22 **Being ... credit** Who consist entirely of trust; i.e. we are entirely ready to believe.

23 Compare 2.2.165 where Adriana has declared that she will fasten on her husband's sleeve as a vine upon an elm.

24 **motion** orbit; the term is picked up from the motions of heavenly bodies.

27 **vain** false (Onions); referring to 'the sweet breath of flattery [which] conquers strife' in the following line.

32 **earth's wonder** Perhaps intended as a compliment to Queen Elizabeth. The Chamber Accounts list payments to Shakespeare, Kemp, and Richard Burbage on behalf of their company of players on 26 and 28 December 1594. See p. 28 above.

Teach me, dear creature, how to think and speak.
  Lay open to my earthy gross conceit,
Smothered in errors, feeble, shallow, weak,   35
  The folded meaning of your words' deceit.
Against my soul's pure truth why labour you
  To make it wander in an unknown field?
Are you a god? Would you create me new?
  Transform me, then, and to your power I'll yield.   40
But if that I am I, then well I know
  Your weeping sister is no wife of mine,
Nor to her bed no homage do I owe.
  Far more, far more to you do I decline.
O, train me not, sweet mermaid, with thy note   45
  To drown me in thy sister's flood of tears.
Sing, siren, for thyself, and I will dote.
  Spread o'er the silver waves thy golden hairs
And as a bed I'll take thee, and there lie,
  And in that glorious supposition think   50
He gains by death that hath such means to die.
  Let love, being light, be drownèd if she sink.
LUCIANA What, are you mad, that you do reason so?

46 sister's] F2; sister F   49 bed] F2; bud F

34 **earthy gross conceit** earth-bound understanding. Platonic teaching, partly assimilated into Christian tradition, held that the truth remained obscure to us in the flesh but would be revealed when we are released from it into the 'soul's pure truth' (37). Shakespeare is admitting another kind of divided self (the gross and the pure). For the Platonic vision of man compare *MV* 5.1.64: 'this muddy vesture of decay'. In the ordinary world, however, Antipholus hopes that Luciana will make sense of what look to him like lies ('words' deceit').
35 **Smothered in errors** As the play is.
36 **folded** hidden.
37–8 Why do you struggle to make my pure and constant soul wander into the field of infidelity that it knows nothing about?
44 **decline** incline (to Luciana rather than to Adriana).
45–52 The succession of water images ('mermaid', 'drown', 'flood', 'siren', 'waves', 'drowned', 'sink') recalls the use of such imagery to denote insecurity, loss of identity – by Antipholus S. (1.2.35–40), by Adriana (2.2.116–20). Here it is represented rather as a state that is desirable to a lover.

45 **train** entice; compare *LLL* 1.1.71: 'train our intellects to vain delights'.
45 **mermaid** siren; as in *The Rape of Lucrece* 1411; compare 'siren' two lines lower, and 'note' (= music). 'Siren' perhaps suggests that he feels himself inescapably lured.
49 **bed** This emendation of F 'bud' seems inevitable in view of the following 'there lie'. It appears already in F2, which renders unlikely Foakes's inclination to retain 'bud' (= a maid – compare *Rom.* 2.2.29 and *The Rape of Lucrece* 848), taking 'hairs' as the antecedent of 'there'. Either way it is not a happy image.
51 **die** Perhaps carries the connotation of 'die' as a term for the consummation of love.
52 **light** A play on the two senses of 'buoyant' and 'wanton'. The line as a whole suggests Antipholus's love for Luciana, combined with his suspicion of her as a siren luring him to his death.
53 Antipholus's lyrical quatrains give place here to keen single-line exchanges (stichomythia). See 2.1.0 SD n., and compare *R3* 1.2.131–50, 192–202.

ANTIPHOLUS S. Not mad, but mated. How I do not know.

LUCIANA It is a fault that springeth from your eye.   55

ANTIPHOLUS S. For gazing on your beams, fair sun, being by.

LUCIANA Gaze where you should, and that will clear your sight.

ANTIPHOLUS S. As good to wink, sweet love, as look on night.

LUCIANA Why call you me 'love'? Call my sister so.

ANTIPHOLUS S. Thy sister's sister.

LUCIANA   That's my sister.

ANTIPHOLUS S.   No,   60
    It is thyself, mine own self's better part,
    Mine eye's clear eye, my dear heart's dearer heart,
    My food, my fortune, and my sweet hope's aim,
    My sole earth's heaven, and my heaven's claim.

LUCIANA All this my sister is, or else should be.   65

ANTIPHOLUS S. Call thyself sister, sweet, for I am thee.
    Thee will I love, and with thee lead my life.
    Thou hast no husband yet, nor I no wife.
    Give me thy hand.

LUCIANA   O soft, sir, hold you still.
    I'll fetch my sister to get her good will.   *Exit*   70

Enter DROMIO OF SYRACUSE

ANTIPHOLUS S. Why, how now, Dromio. Where runnest thou so fast?

DROMIO S. Do you know me sir? Am I Dromio? Am I your man? Am I myself?

ANTIPHOLUS S. Thou art Dromio, thou art my man, thou art thyself.

DROMIO S. I am an ass, I am a woman's man, and besides myself.   75

ANTIPHOLUS S. What woman's man? And how besides thyself?

DROMIO S. Marry, sir, besides myself I am due to a woman, one that claims me, one that haunts me, one that will have me.

---

57 where] *Rowe²*; when F

---

54 mated (1) confounded; (2) amazed; (3) mated as husband and wife. All three senses seem to be implied.

55 fault Luciana takes Antipholus's sudden declaration of love as an offence, mere lust awakened by gazing on her beauty.

58 wink close one's eyes; the normal Elizabethan meaning.

61 mine . . . part Adriana had earlier (2.2.114) used almost identical words to Antipholus, who here applies them to Luciana.

64 My only heaven on earth, and my (only) claim on heaven.

66 Call yourself your sister, sweet one, for I am part of you – as you think I should be of her. This picks up the thought of 61.

70 good will approval. Is this line intended as a stratagem enabling Luciana to escape Antipholus's unwelcome advances, or is she finding herself attracted to him, as is suggested in her words to Adriana in 4.2.14–16?

75–8 Dromio's situation in this episode is a burlesque of his master's. Each in his own way has become 'a woman's man' and is therefore 'besides himself' – yet another way the play finds to describe a split self.

75 besides myself A quibble: 'out of my wits'; 'myself as well'.

ANTIPHOLUS S. What claim lays she to thee?

DROMIO S. Marry, sir, such claim as you would lay to your horse; and   80
she would have me as a beast – not that, I being a beast, she would
have me, but that she, being a very beastly creature, lays claim to
me.

ANTIPHOLUS S. What is she?

DROMIO S. A very reverend body; ay, such a one as a man may not   85
speak of without he say 'sir-reverence'. I have but lean luck in the
match, and yet is she a wondrous fat marriage.

ANTIPHOLUS S. How dost thou mean, a fat marriage?

DROMIO S. Marry, sir, she's the kitchen wench, and all grease; and I
know not what use to put her to but to make a lamp of her and run   90
from her by her own light. I warrant her rags and the tallow in them
will burn a Poland winter. If she lives till doomsday she'll burn a
week longer than the whole world.

ANTIPHOLUS S. What complexion is she of?

DROMIO S. Swart like my shoe, but her face nothing like so clean kept.   95
For why? She sweats a man may go overshoes in the grime of it.

ANTIPHOLUS S. That's a fault that water will mend.

DROMIO S. No, sir, 'tis in grain. Noah's flood could not do it.

ANTIPHOLUS S. What's her name?

DROMIO S. Nell, sir. But her name and three quarters – that's an ell and   100
three quarters – will not measure her from hip to hip.

ANTIPHOLUS S. Then she bears some breadth?

DROMIO S. No longer from head to foot than from hip to hip. She is
spherical, like a globe; I could find out countries in her.

ANTIPHOLUS S. In what part of her body stands Ireland.   105

DROMIO S. Marry, sir, in her buttocks. I found it out by the bogs.

ANTIPHOLUS S. Where Scotland?

---

100 name and] *Conj. Theobald, Thirlby;* name is F

81–2 Editors, not very plausibly, suggest that there is a quibble on 'a beast' and 'abased', and that 'have' has a sexual connotation.

86 **sir-reverence** A corruption of 'save your reverence', a phrase of respect prefacing something that might cause offence.

89 **grease** A quibble on 'grace'. But 'grease' is apt in the context.

92 **Poland winter** Suggests a long, dark, northern European winter.

93 **a week** NS and others suggest a pun on 'wick'.

94–124 For this catalogue compare *TGV* 3.1.293 ff., and Lyly's *Midas* 1.2.19 ff.

95 **Swart** Swarthy, dark.

96 **sweats a man** sweats so much that a man.

96 **overshoes** Proverbial for 'over the shoes', 'deeply immersed'. See Tilley s380.

98 **in grain** ingrained; compare *TN* 1.5.235: ''Tis in grain, sir, 'twill endure wind and weather.'

100 **Nell** Probably the same person as Luce, here referred to as Nell for the sake of the pun, 'an ell'.

100 **ell** The English ell is 45 inches.

106 **bogs** Probably a quibble, with connotations of 'privy'. *OED* does not help.

DROMIO S. I found it by the barrenness, hard in the palm of the hand.

ANTIPHOLUS S. Where France?

DROMIO S. In her forehead, armed and reverted, making war against   110
her heir.

ANTIPHOLUS S. Where England?

DROMIO S. I looked for the chalky cliffs, but I could find no whiteness
in them. But I guess it stood in her chin, by the salt rheum that ran
between France and it.   115

ANTIPHOLUS S. Where Spain?

DROMIO S. Faith, I saw it not, but I felt it hot in her breath.

ANTIPHOLUS S. Where America, the Indies?

DROMIO S. O, sir, upon her nose, all o'er embellished with rubies,
carbuncles, sapphires, declining their rich aspect to the hot breath   120
of Spain, who sent whole armadoes of carracks to be ballast at her
nose.

ANTIPHOLUS S. Where stood Belgia, the Netherlands?

DROMIO S. O, sir, I did not look so low. To conclude, this drudge or
diviner laid claim to me, called me Dromio, swore I was assured to   125
her, told me what privy marks I had about me, as the mark of my
shoulder, the mole in my neck, the great wart on my left arm, that I,
amazed, ran from her as a witch.

And I think if my breast had not been made of faith, and my
heart of steel,
She had transformed me to a curtal dog, and made me turn
i'the wheel.   130

ANTIPHOLUS S. Go, hie thee presently. Post to the road.

111 heir] F (heire); haire F2   113 chalky] F2; chalkle F   121 carracks] *Hanmer*; Carrects F

109–11 The relevance of this passage to the
dating of the play is discussed at pp. 1–2 above.
There is a pun in 'heir'; Johnson suggested that
'reverted' represents the hair ('heir') receding, or
falling out, as a result of venereal disease, and
'armed' the scabs of the chancres caused by the
same disease.

113 **chalky cliffs** i.e. teeth; compare the white
cliffs of Dover.

114 **salt rheum** The discharge from the nose
(? or eyes), representing the English Channel.

116–22 **Spain . . . nose** The comparison of
her nose to Spain alludes to her red and blue
eruptions and her hot and smelly breath, to the
jewelled wealth of Spain, its climate, and its spice
trade with America and the East Indies. Dromio
pictures armed fleets (armadas) of galleons or
large merchant ships (carracks) taking on ballast
from her dripping nostrils. 'Armado' was the

usual spelling of 'Armada'; 'ballast' is a past participle. This is Shakespeare's only direct reference
to America.

123–4 **Netherlands . . . low** He did not look
at the nether parts of her body.

125 **diviner** witch, magician; compare 140.

125 **assured** betrothed.

129–30 **And . . . wheel** Foakes suggests, I
think rightly, that this couplet (prose in F) is an
echo of Ephes. 6.11 ff.: 'Put on all the armour of
God, that yee may stande against the assaults of
the deuill . . . hauing on the breast plate of
righteousnesse . . . the shelde of faith . . .'

130 **curtal dog** A dog with a docked tail.

130 **turn i'the wheel** tread a wheel to turn a
spit. Proverbial; see Tilley M87.

131 **presently** immediately.

131 **Post . . . road** Hurry to the anchorage.

And if the wind blow any way from shore
I will not harbour in this town tonight.
If any bark put forth, come to the mart,
Where I will walk till thou return to me.   135
If everyone knows us, and we know none,
'Tis time, I think, to trudge, pack, and be gone.

DROMIO S. As from a bear a man would run for life,
   So fly I from her that would be my wife.   *Exit*

ANTIPHOLUS S. There's none but witches do inhabit here,   140
   And therefore 'tis high time that I were hence.
   She that doth call me husband, even my soul
   Doth for a wife abhor. But her fair sister,
   Possessed with such a gentle sovereign grace,
   Of such enchanting presence and discourse,   145
   Hath almost made me traitor to myself.
   But lest myself be guilty to self-wrong,
   I'll stop mine ears against the mermaid's song.

Enter ANGELO *with the chain*

ANGELO Master Antipholus.
                     Ay, that's my name.
ANGELO I know it well, sir. Lo, here's the chain.   150
   I thought to have ta'en you at the Porpentine.
   The chain unfinished made me stay thus long.
ANTIPHOLUS S. What is your will that I shall do with this?
ANGELO What please yourself, sir. I have made it for you.
ANTIPHOLUS S. Made it for me, sir? I bespoke it not.   155
ANGELO Not once, nor twice, but twenty times you have.
   Go home with it, and please your wife withal,
   And soon at supper-time I'll visit you,
   And then receive my money for the chain.
ANTIPHOLUS S. I pray you, sir, receive the money now,   160

141 high] hie F

132 **And if** If.
138–41 The parallel between master and slave is very close here, each fleeing from a woman – the one a woman who is repulsive, the other a woman who is (hitherto) adorable. Antipholus is even willing to renounce his love for Luciana. She may be part of the witchcraft by which he seems to be surrounded; he calls her 'mermaid' twice, at 45 above, and again at 148, and the word 'enchanting' (145) may be taken in two senses.

148 In the *Odyssey* (Bk 12) Odysseus had to stop the ears of his crew with wax to prevent them from being enchanted by the Sirens.
151 **ta'en . . . Porpentine** overtaken you at the Porcupine.
154 **What please yourself** What it may please you.

For fear you ne'er see chain nor money more.

ANGELO You are a merry man, sir. Fare you well.   *Exit*

ANTIPHOLUS S. What I should think of this I cannot tell.

But this I think, there's no man is so vain

That would refuse so fair an offered chain.   165

I see a man here needs not live by shifts,

When in the streets he meets such golden gifts.

I'll to the mart, and there for Dromio stay;

If any ship put out, then straight away.   *Exit*

4.1 *Enter a* [SECOND] MERCHANT, [ANGELO *the*] *goldsmith, and an*
OFFICER

2 MERCHANT You know since Pentecost the sum is due,

And since I have not much importuned you;

Nor now I had not, but that I am bound

To Persia, and want guilders for my voyage.

Therefore make present satisfaction,   5

Or I'll attach you by this officer.

ANGELO Even just the sum that I do owe to you

Is growing to me by Antipholus,

And in the instant that I met with you

He had of me a chain. At five o'clock   10

I shall receive the money for the same.

Pleaseth you walk with me down to his house,

I will discharge my bond, and thank you too.

Act 4, Scene 1   4.1] *Actus Quartus. Scæna Prima* F   0 SD] *Enter a Merchant, Goldsmith, and an Officer.* F   1 SH
2MERCHANT] *Mar.* F   7 SH ANGELO] *Gold.* F *(throughout scene)*

164 **vain** foolish.
166 **shifts** tricks.
169 **straight** immediately.

Act 4, Scene 1

0 SD SECOND The F stage direction does not
distinguish this Merchant from the one in 1.2,
who knows all about Ephesus, whereas the
present Merchant has to ask (5.1.4) how Antipholus E. is reputed. In this short blank-verse
scene the comedy of the confusions and frustra-
tions introduces a tone of hostility and violence.

1 **Pentecost** Whitsuntide; another Christian
term in this 'Roman' comedy.

4 **guilders** See 1.1.8 n.
5 **present satisfaction** immediate payment.
6 **attach** arrest.
8 **growing** due.
10 **five o'clock** Several references point to five
o'clock as the hour at which the action will be
completed: 1.2.26; 3.2.158 ('soon at supper-
time', which was normally five o'clock); the
present mention; 5.1.118 ('the dial points at
five').
12 **Pleaseth you** May it please you.

Enter ANTIPHOLUS OF EPHESUS [*and*] DROMIO [OF EPHESUS] *from the*
Courtesan's

OFFICER That labour may you save. See where he comes.

ANTIPHOLUS E. While I go to the goldsmith's house, go thou   15
    And buy a rope's end; that will I bestow
    Among my wife and her confederates
    For locking me out of my doors by day.
    But soft, I see the goldsmith. Get thee gone.
    Buy thou a rope, and bring it home to me.   20
DROMIO E. I buy a thousand pound a year, I buy a rope.   *Exit*
ANTIPHOLUS E. A man is well help up that trusts to you.
    I promisèd your presence and the chain,
    But neither chain nor goldsmith came to me.
    Belike you thought our love would last too long   25
    If it were chained together, and therefore came not.
ANGELO Saving your merry humour, here's the note
    How much your chain weighs to the utmost carat,
    The fineness of the gold, and chargeful fashion,
    Which doth amount to three odd ducats more   30
    Than I stand debted to this gentleman.
    I pray you see him presently discharged,
    For he is bound to sea, and stays but for it.
ANTIPHOLUS E. I am not furnished with the present money;
    Besides, I have some business in the town.   35
    Good signior, take the stranger to my house,
    And with you take the chain, and bid my wife
    Disburse the sum on the receipt thereof.

13 SD *Enter* ANTIPHOLUS OF EPHESUS *and* DROMIO OF EPHESUS] *Enter Antipholus Ephes. Dromio* F   28 carat]
charect F

13 SD This supports the conjecture that for this
play there would have been – at any rate when
performed in halls – three separate houses from
which entry to the stage could be made – in this
case presumably a house marked with the sign of
a porcupine.
  21 What is the point of this joke – as it is
obviously intended to be? Is Dromio saying that,
in buying the wherewithal to punish those who
locked him and his master out of the house, he is
buying something very valuable? If he is referring
to the beatings that he himself so often receives,
'marks', as elsewhere in the play, would perhaps
have made a more immediately grasped quibble

than 'pound'; but at *TGV* 1.1.103–7 'pound' is
punningly used to signify both a beating and a
pinfold.
  22 holp up helped; a frequent form.
  25 Belike Perhaps.
  27 Saving With regard to.
  29 chargeful fashion costly workmanship.
  30 ducats Gold coins the value of which varied
from country to country.
  32 presently immediately; compare 'present'
(34).

Perchance I will be there as soon as you.
ANGELO Then you will bring the chain to her yourself.   40
ANTIPHOLUS E. No, bear it with you lest I come not time enough.
ANGELO Well, sir, I will. Have you the chain about you?
ANTIPHOLUS E. And if I have not, sir, I hope you have,
   Or else you may return without your money.
ANGELO Nay, come, I pray you, sir, give me the chain.   45
   Both wind and tide stays for this gentleman,
   And I, to blame, have held him here too long.
ANTIPHOLUS E. Good lord, you use this dalliance to excuse
   Your breach of promise to the Porpentine.
   I should have chid you for not bringing it,   50
   But like a shrew you first begin to brawl.
2 MERCHANT The hour steals on. I pray you, sir, dispatch.
ANGELO You hear how he importunes me. The chain!
ANTIPHOLUS E. Why, give it to my wife, and fetch your money.
ANGELO Come, come. You know I gave it you even now.   55
   Either send the chain, or send me by some token.
ANTIPHOLUS E. Fie, now you run this humour out of breath.
   Come, where's the chain? I pray you let me see it.
2 MERCHANT My business cannot brook this dalliance.
   Good sir, say whe'er you'll answer me or no.   60
   If not, I'll leave him to the officer.
ANTIPHOLUS E. I answer you? What should I answer you?
ANGELO The money that you owe me for the chain.
ANTIPHOLUS E. I owe you none till I receive the chain.
ANGELO You know I gave it you half an hour since.   65
ANTIPHOLUS E. You gave me none. You wrong me much to say so.
ANGELO You wrong me more, sir, in denying it.
   Consider how it stands upon my credit.
2 MERCHANT Well, officer, arrest him at my suit.
OFFICER   I do,

52, 59, 69 SH 2MERCHANT] *Mar.* F   56 me by] F; *by me Alexander (Singer subst.)*   69–70] *As Capell; prose in* F

41 **time enough** in time, soon enough.
46 A reminiscence of the proverb, 'Time and tide wait for no man'; see Tilley T283.
47 **to blame** Some editors retain the F 'too blame' (F3 'to blame'); in the sixteenth and seventeenth centuries 'blame' could mean 'blameworthy' (*OED* Blame *v* 6).
51 **shrew** Normally used for a person of either sex. Lines 50–1 embrace the proverb, 'Some complain to prevent complaint' (Tilley C579).

Compare *R3* 1.3.324: 'I do the wrong and first begin to brawl.'
56 **send me . . . token** send to me with some evidence (of my right to receive payment).
57 **run . . . breath** carry this joke too far.
60 **whe'er** whether; a frequent form in Shakespeare – here alone F reads 'whe'r'.
60 **answer** give me satisfaction.
64 **chain** The insistent repetition of the word may perhaps recall to us Othello's importunate demands for the handkerchief (*Oth.* 3.4.51–98).

And charge you in the Duke's name to obey me.   70
ANGELO This touches me in reputation.
    Either consent to pay this sum for me,
    Or I attach you by this officer.
ANTIPHOLUS E. Consent to pay thee that I never had?
    Arrest me, foolish fellow, if thou dar'st.   75
ANGELO Here is thy fee. Arrest him, officer.
    I would not spare my brother in this case
    If he should scorn me so apparently.
OFFICER I do arrest you, sir. You hear the suit.
ANTIPHOLUS E. I do obey thee till I give thee bail.   80
    But, sirrah, you shall buy this sport as dear
    As all the metal in your shop will answer.
ANGELO Sir, sir, I shall have law in Ephesus,
    To your notorious shame, I doubt it not.

Enter DROMIO OF SYRACUSE *from the bay*

DROMIO S. Master, there's a bark of Epidamnum   85
    That stays but till her owner comes aboard,
    And then she bears away. Our fraughtage, sir,
    I have conveyed aboard, and I have bought
    The oil, the balsamum, and aqua-vitae.
    The ship is in her trim; the merry wind   90
    Blows fair from land. They stay for naught at all
    But for their owner, master, and yourself.
ANTIPHOLUS E. How now? A madman? Why, thou peevish sheep,
    What ship of Epidamnum stays for me?
DROMIO S. A ship you sent me to, to hire waftage.   95
ANTIPHOLUS E. Thou drunken slave, I sent thee for a rope,

87 then she] *Capell;* then sir she F

76 **fee** Public officers were entitled to a fee for carrying out their duties.

78 **apparently** obviously.

81 **sirrah** Editors have noted Antipholus's increasing distrust and scorn in his forms of address to Angelo: 'Good signior', 'sir', 'fellow', 'sirrah'.

84 SD The words 'from the bay' (F) suggest an entry to the stage (the mart) from the side, as it were from a road, at one end of the postulated three-house stage set.

87 **fraughtage** freight, baggage.

89 **balsamum** balm, a fragrant and healing resin; the only occasion on which Shakespeare uses the Latin form.

89 **aqua-vitae** alcoholic spirits. Were these two commodities regarded as specifics against sea-sickness, or aids to recovery from sea-sickness?

90 **in her trim** fully rigged and ready to sail.

92 **master** Is Dromio addressing Antipholus, or is he referring to the ship's master (captain), as distinct from the owner?

93 **peevish** senseless. 'Sheep' in this line and 'ship' in the next are very probably intended as a pun; compare *TGV* 1.1.72–3. 'Madman' reminds us how often in this play (as in farces generally) characters regard other people (or themselves) as madmen.

And told thee to what purpose, and what end.

DROMIO S. You sent me for a rope's end as soon.

You sent me to the bay, sir, for a bark.

ANTIPHOLUS E. I will debate this matter at more leisure,   100

And teach your ears to list me with more heed.

To Adriana, villain, hie thee straight.

Give her this key, and tell her in the desk

That's covered o'er with Turkish tapestry

There is a purse of ducats. Let her send it.   105

Tell her I am arrested in the street,

And that shall bail me. Hie thee, slave. Be gone.

On, officer, to prison, till it come.

Exeunt [all but Dromio of Syracuse]

DROMIO S. To Adriana. That is where we dined,

Where Dowsabel did claim me for her husband.   110

She is too big, I hope, for me to compass.

Thither I must, although against my will;

For servants must their masters' minds fulfil.   *Exit*

4.2   *Enter* ADRIANA *and* LUCIANA

ADRIANA Ah, Luciana, did he tempt thee so?

Mightst thou perceive austerely in his eye

That he did plead in earnest, yea or no?

108 SD *all but Dromio of Syracuse*] *Not in* F   **Act 4, Scene 2**   4.2] *Capell; not in* F

98 **rope's end** whipping. It was Dromio E. who was sent to buy a rope's end (16).

104 **Turkish tapestry** Needlework with a pattern imitating an oriental carpet.

110 **Dowsabel** Derived from the Italian 'Dulcibella', or the French 'douce et belle', and used as the name of a sweetheart or pretty girl, as in Cotton, *Scoffer Scoft* (1675), 75: 'give me her as my Dowsabel'; also a rustic name in pastorals, as in Drayton, *Eglogue* iv, 125–6: 'He had as antike stories tell / A daughter cleaped Dowsabel.' Here used ironically of Nell.

111 **compass** (1) embrace; (2) win.

Act 4, Scene 2

4.2 This scene carries on from the scene of Antipholus's wooing of Luciana (3.2), which itself carries on from the earlier Luciana–Adriana

exchange on marital relations (2.1); here, however, Luciana's revelations lead to deeper impatience and disillusion in Adriana, though the moment she hears that Antipholus (it is her own Antipholus, of course) is in trouble, her deep love for him again rises above all other feelings. We have the by now familiar Luciana–Adriana verse-idiom. The dialogue, picking up from 3.2.70, begins with a rhymed sestet, carries on with (largely) rhymed stichomythia, and is brought to a close with a further rhymed passage, followed, on the entry of Dromio S., by more, livelier, rhymed stichomythia and longer rhymed speeches. Adriana and Luciana enter, we must assume, from their house, the Phoenix, on one side of the stage.

2 **austerely** Compare 'in earnest' in the following line.

Looked he or red or pale, or sad or merrily?
What observation mad'st thou in this case   5
Of his heart's meteors tilting in his face?

LUCIANA First, he denied you had in him no right.

ADRIANA He meant he did me none, the more my spite.

LUCIANA Then swore he that he was a stranger here.

ADRIANA And true he swore, though yet forsworn he were.   10

LUCIANA Then pleaded I for you.

ADRIANA   And what said he?

LUCIANA That love I begged for you, he begged of me.

ADRIANA With what persuasion did he tempt thy love?

LUCIANA With words that in an honest suit might move.

First he did praise my beauty, then my speech.   15

ADRIANA Didst speak him fair?

LUCIANA   Have patience, I beseech.

ADRIANA I cannot nor I will not hold me still.
My tongue, though not my heart, shall have his will.
He is deformèd, crooked, old, and sere;
Ill-faced, worse-bodied, shapeless everywhere;   20
Vicious, ungentle, foolish, blunt, unkind,
Stigmatical in making, worse in mind.

LUCIANA Who would be jealous, then, of such a one?
No evil lost is wailed when it is gone.

ADRIANA Ah, but I think him better than I say,   25
And yet would herein others' eyes were worse.
Far from her nest the lapwing cries away.
My heart prays for him, though my tongue do curse.

5–6 case / Of] F2; case? / Oh, F

4 **or sad or merrily** This phrase is used also at *1H4* 5.2.12; 'sad' = serious, as at 3.1.19.
6 **heart's ... face** conflicting emotions as shown in his face. Any luminous manifestation in the heavens might be termed a 'meteor'; compare *Rom.* 3.5.13. 'Tilting' suggests the emotions fighting, as if at a jousting.
7 **no** The double negative, as often in Shakespeare, intensifies the negative; see Abbott 406.
8 **spite** vexation.
14 **honest suit** honourable courtship; as indeed it was, in spite of appearances.
18 **his** its; the normal genitive of 'it' until late in Shakespeare's career.

19 **sere** withered, dried up.
20 **shapeless** unshapely.
21 **ungentle** lacking in noble qualities.
22 **Stigmatical in making** Deformed in aspect – in the way he is made; compare pejorative sense of 'stigma'.
26 **others' ... worse** i.e. they would not see his faults. She is in effect admitting that she still loves him, as she declares more specifically in 28.
27 **lapwing** A reference to the lapwing's practice of drawing intruders away from the nest to protect her nestlings. The image brings out the difference between what Adriana says and what she feels.

Enter DROMIO OF SYRACUSE

DROMIO S. Here, go – the desk, the purse, sweat now, make haste.
LUCIANA How hast thou lost thy breath?
DROMIO S.   By running fast.   30
ADRIANA Where is thy master, Dromio? Is he well?
DROMIO S. No. He's in Tartar limbo, worse than hell.
 A devil in an everlasting garment hath him,
 One whose hard heart is buttoned up with steel,
 A fiend, a fairy, pitiless and rough;   35
 A wolf, nay, worse, a fellow all in buff;
 A backfriend, a shoulder-clapper, one that countermands
 The passages of alleys, creeks, and narrow lands;
 A hound that runs counter, and yet draws dryfoot well;
 One that before the Judgement carries poor souls to hell.   40
ADRIANA Why, man, what is the matter?
DROMIO S. I do not know the matter, he is 'rested on the case.

29 sweat now] *NS;* sweet now F   34 One] F2; On F   35 rough] F (ruffe)   42, 45 'rested] *Theobald;* rested F

29 sweat F reads 'sweet now make haste'. 'Sweat' is adopted by most editors; perhaps the compositor read MS. *swet(e)* as 'sweet'. The line represents Dromio's incoherence as he enters in a violent hurry, and the reading 'sweat' accords well with the breathlessness induced in him 'by running fast'.

32 Tartar limbo 'Limbo' was often used for a prison (*OED* 2), and also for hell (*OED* 2c), though strictly speaking it is a region bordering on hell. Here it clearly means 'prison', though hell is implied. 'Tartar(us)' was the infernal prison of classical mythology; some of the audience may have read into it also an allusion to the savage Tartars.

33 everlasting A material used for the uniform of sergeants and catchpoles (*OED* sv *sb* 3a).

35 fairy Until Shakespeare later transformed them, fairies were often regarded as malevolent, at best mischievous beings. Shakespeare gives Puck some of the mischievous attributes of the traditional fairies. The frequent emendation to 'fury' is not necessary.

36 buff A hard-wearing material used for the uniforms of sergeants and other legal officials; compare 'everlasting' above.

37 backfriend ... shoulder-clapper Ironic references to an arresting officer or bailiff, who is like a friend who claps one on the back or shoulder ('backfriend' normally means one who,

while hating you, pretends to be your friend, and 'shoulder-clapper' became a slang term for an arresting officer); 'countermands' means 'inhibits', probably with a pun on the Counter, a name for various debtors' prisons of the time.

38 i.e. the movement of people in narrow places. 'Lands' has not been explained, but perhaps means 'glades', or small clearings (compare 'launds'), or just stretches of land like the fields round London; 'creeks' here means 'winding lanes' (*OED* Creek *sb*¹ 5).

39 hound ... counter hound that runs in a direction opposite to that taken by the game; with a quibble on 'counter' (37); 'draws dryfoot' is a hunting term which means tracking game by the 'mere scent of the foot' (*OED* Dry-foot *adv* 2).

40 Two puns: one on judgement in the courts, and on the Day of Judgement; the other on hell in its literal sense, and on a well-known debtors' prison in Westminster – compare Thomas Fuller, *Worthies of England* (1662), II, 236, under proverbs of Westminster, 'There is no redemption from Hell': 'There is a place partly under, partly by the *Exchequer Court* commonly called Hell . . . I am informed that formerly this place was appointed a prison for the Kings debtors . . .'

41 matter Probably with the legal implication, 'allegation', 'matter to be proved'.

42 the case A legal term referring to arrests not specifically covered by normal procedures.

ADRIANA What, is he arrested? Tell me at whose suit.

DROMIO S. I know not at whose suit he is arrested well;
But is in a suit of buff which 'rested him, that can I tell.   45
Will you send him, mistress, redemption, the money in his
    desk?

ADRIANA Go fetch it, sister.

Exit Luciana

                    This I wonder at,
That he unknown to me should be in debt.
Tell me, was he arrested on a band?

DROMIO S. Not on a band, but on a stronger thing: 50
A chain, a chain – do you not hear it ring?

ADRIANA What, the chain?

DROMIO S. No, no, the bell. 'Tis time that I were gone.
It was two ere I left him, and now the clock strikes one.

ADRIANA The hours come back; that did I never hear.   55

DROMIO S. O yes, if any hour meet a sergeant 'a turns back for very
    fear.

ADRIANA As if time were in debt. How fondly dost thou reason!

DROMIO S. Time is a very bankrupt, and owes more than he's worth to
    season.
Nay, he's a thief, too. Have you not heard men say
That time comes stealing on by night and day?   60
If 'a be in debt and theft, and a sergeant in the way,
Hath he not reason to turn back an hour in a day?

44–6] *As Capell; as prose,* F 46 mistress, redemption,] *Hanmer;* Mistris redemption, F; Mistris Redemption, F4
48 That] F2; thus F 56 'a] *Staunton;* I F; Time *Rowe;* he *Malone*

46 **redemption** ransom, the means to redeem himself.

49, 50 band A pun on 'bond' (an alternative spelling) and 'band' as a neck-band, alluding to the chain in 51.

53–4 'tis time . . . strikes one There is a good deal of (? deliberate) confusion of time in the play. Is it possible that 'strikes one' refers to the priory bell striking some hour?

56 **sergeant** The legal official who arrests offenders, or summons them to court; compare the 'shoulder-clapper' of 37. H. Kökeritz, *Shakespeare's Pronunciation*, 1953, p. 117, plausibly suggests a pun, 'hour/whore', in this line.

57 **fondly** foolishly; as is normal in Shakespeare.

58 A difficult line, meaning perhaps, 'Time has overspent itself, and it's more trouble than it's worth to set its affairs straight', or '. . . and owes so much that he's not worth holding on to'. Kökeritz (p. 114) suggests that there is a pun between 'season' and 'seisin', a legal term used in phrases denoting 'possession', 'keeping possession' (spelt 'season' in a quotation from 1523 in *OED*). I think this very likely. For the many law terms in this episode (32–61) see the comments on the legal imagery and terminology in the play at pp. 19–20 above.

59 Proverbial; see Tilley T313, 327.

61–2 **If . . . day** If time is in debt, and a thief as well, and encounters a sergeant, hasn't he good reason to turn back to the extent of an hour a day? See 53–4.

Enter LUCIANA

ADRIANA Go, Dromio, there's the money. Bear it straight,
And bring thy master home immediately.
Come, sister, I am pressed down with conceit –   65
Conceit, my comfort and my injury.

Exeunt

4.3 *Enter* ANTIPHOLUS OF SYRACUSE

ANTIPHOLUS S. There's not a man I meet but doth salute me
As if I were their well-acquainted friend,
And every one doth call me by my name.
Some tender money to me, some invite me,
Some other give me thanks for kindnesses.   5
Some offer me commodities to buy.
Even now a tailor called me in his shop
And showed me silks that he had bought for me,
And therewithal took measure of my body.
Sure, these are but imaginary wiles,   10
And Lapland sorcerers inhabit here.

Enter DROMIO OF SYRACUSE

DROMIO S. Master, here's the gold you sent me for. What, have you got
the picture of old Adam new-apparelled?
ANTIPHOLUS S. What gold is this? What Adam dost thou mean?

Act 4, Scene 3   4.3] *Capell; not in* F   0 SD OF SYRACUSE] *Siracusia* F   1 SH ANTIPHOLUS S.] *Not in* F   11 SD *of Syracuse*] *Sir.* F   12 What, have] *Rowe²; what haue* F

65 pressed down oppressed, burdened.
65 conceit imagination (both of the injury done to her and of the comfort she can bring to her husband).
66 SD Presumably Adriana and Luciana go back into their home, while Dromio runs off to relieve his master.

Act 4, Scene 3
4.3 With the entry of the Courtesan the comedy of errors is further intensified and complicated, especially for Antipholus of Syracuse.
5 other A normal plural (see Abbott 12).
10 imaginary wiles tricks of the imagination.
11 Lapland sorcerers Lapland was proverbially the home of witches and sorcerers; compare Giles Fletcher, *Of the Russe Common Wealth* (1591): 'For practice of witchcraft and sorcery they [i.e. the Lapps] pass all nations in the world.'

12–13 What ... new-apparelled? The general sense seems to be 'What, have you got rid of that sinful fellow the sergeant?' Dromio has a few minutes earlier seen Antipholus E. arrested, and sees him now (as he thinks) alone and at liberty. There is a pun in 'new-apparelled'. The 'old Adam' – i.e. the sergeant – represents 'th'offending Adam' (compare *H5* 1.1.29), man in his fallen state, and Dromio suggests either, or both, that he has changed from his buff garments and therefore ceased to be a sergeant and gone off, or that (taking apparel as 'suit' in its legal sense) he has gone off to deal with a new offender. There are two oblique biblical allusions: to Eph. 4.22–4, 'To lay down ... the old man, which is corrupt ... And to put on that new man, which after God is shapen in righteousnes' (see Appendix 2, p. 113 below); and to Gen. 3.21, 'Unto Adam also and to his wife did the Lord God make coats of skin, and clothed them.'

DROMIO S. Not that Adam that kept the paradise, but that Adam that   15
keeps the prison. He that goes in the calf's skin that was killed for
the prodigal. He that came behind you, sir, like an evil angel, and
bid you forsake your liberty.

ANTIPHOLUS S. I understand thee not.

DROMIO S. No? Why, 'tis a plain case: he that went like a bass viol in a   20
case of leather; the man, sir, that when gentlemen are tired gives
them a sob and rests them; he, sir, that takes pity on decayed men
and gives them suits of durance; he that sets up his rest to do more
exploits with his mace than a morris-pike.

ANTIPHOLUS S. What, thou meanest an officer?   25

DROMIO S. Ay, sir, the sergeant of the band; he that brings any man to
answer it that breaks his band; one that thinks a man always going to
bed, and says, 'God give you good rest.'

ANTIPHOLUS S. Well, sir, there rest in your foolery. Is there any ships
puts forth tonight? May we be gone?   30

DROMIO S. Why, sir, I brought you word an hour since that the bark
Expedition put forth tonight, and then were you hindered by the
sergeant to tarry for the hoy Delay. Here are the angels that you sent
for to deliver you.

ANTIPHOLUS S. The fellow is distract, and so am I,   35
    And here we wander in illusions,
    Some blessèd power deliver us from hence!

---

15 the paradise Might this, as Wells suggests, be a topical allusion to an inn kept by a man named Adam?

16–17 the calf's skin ... prodigal Further quibbling. An allusion to the fatted calf killed at the return of the prodigal son (Luke 15.11–32), and at the same time to the leather garments of the sergeant who arrests debtors, those who have been prodigal.

17 evil angel Perhaps another biblical allusion, contrasting the sergeant with the good angel which (Acts 12.5–7) appeared to Peter in prison, struck him on the side, and released him from his bondage.

18 liberty Foakes suggests that we have here a further biblical allusion: 2 Cor. 3.17, 'where the spirit of the Lord is, there is liberty'.

20–1 bass viol ... leather The leather case in which a bass viol is kept; alluding also to the leather garments of the sergeant.

22 sob A breathing-space given to a horse to allow it to recover from its exertions (*OED sb* 1c), punning on the everyday meaning of the word; the pun is picked up in 'rests' and 'rest' in this and the line following, suggesting both respite and arrest.

22 decayed (1) decayed; (2) ruined financially.

23 suits ... rest A pun on hard-wearing cloth suitable for a long term in prison, and on imprisonment. 'Sets up his rest' = 'absolutely determined', a gambling term meaning 'stakes his all' – carrying on the pun on 'rest' and 'arrest'.

24 mace ... morris-pike Contrasts the sergeant's staff of office and the pike ('morris' because of its presumed Moorish origin) as a military weapon.

26 band i.e. of soldiers (or ?law-officers), with an obvious pun on 'band'/'bond' (27). The legal analogies continue.

29 rest The pun again, as at 23.

32–3 Expedition ... Delay Names aptly chosen for the occasion. 'Expedition' = prompt dispatch, and a 'hoy' was a small coasting vessel likely to 'delay' at many ports. An angel was a gold coin, worth, at various times, anything between about 35 and 50 modern pence. Is this coin perhaps chosen here for its biblical connotations?

36 illusions Compare 1.2.97–102, and numerous other passages which demonstrate Antipholus's feeling that he is in a land of illusions and sorceries, and by now needing divine help.

Enter a COURTESAN

COURTESAN Well met, well met, Master Antipholus.
I see, sir, you have found the goldsmith now.
Is that the chain you promised me today?   40
ANTIPHOLUS S. Satan, avoid! I charge thee, tempt me not.
DROMIO S. Master, is this Mistress Satan?
ANTIPHOLUS S. It is the devil.
DROMIO S. Nay, she is worse, she is the devil's dam; and here she
comes in the habit of a light wench; and thereof comes that the   45
wenches say, 'God damn me'; that's as much to say, 'God make me
a light wench.' It is written they appear to men like angels of light.
Light is an effect of fire, and fire will burn. Ergo, light wenches will
burn. Come not near her.
COURTESAN Your man and you are marvellous merry, sir.   50
Will you go with me? We'll mend our dinner here.
DROMIO S. Master, if you do, expect spoon-meat, or bespeak a long
spoon.
ANTIPHOLUS S. Why, Dromio?
DROMIO S. Marry, he must have a long spoon that must eat with the 55
devil.
ANTIPHOLUS S. [*To Courtesan*] Avoid then, fiend. What tell'st thou me
of supping?
Thou art, as you are all, a sorceress.
I conjure thee to leave me and be gone.
COURTESAN Give me the ring of mine you had at dinner,   60

51 with me? . . . here.] *Var. 1778;* with me, . . . here? F   52 you do] F2; do F

37 SD COURTESAN She is not identified in the
dialogue, and she must not be represented as a
common prostitute. (See p. 16 above.) Presumably the audience would identify her by her entry
from her own house, the Porpentine, and perhaps
from some gay quality in her apparel – 'the habit
of a light wench' (45).
41 avoid be off with you; an echo of Christ's
words to Satan at Matt. 4.10: 'Sathan avoid.'
44 devil's dam Literally 'devil's mother', proverbially an opprobrious term for a woman. Tilley
gives several examples (D225), including three
others from Shakespeare.
47 It . . . light 'It is written' is a common biblical phrase, occurring e.g. three times in Matt. 4.
In 2 Cor. 11.14 we read that Satan himself is
transformed into an angel of light, a notion which,

with variations, became proverbial (see Tilley
D231).
48–9 wenches will burn i.e. infect with a
venereal disease.
51 mend complete, add to; 'here' suggests that
the Courtesan indicates her own house.
52–3 spoon-meat . . . long spoon Spoon-
meat is soft food suitable for infants or invalids.
The word is presumably used to introduce the
common proverb, 'He must have a long spoon
that must eat with the devil' in 55–6 (Tilley S771).
'Bespeak' = 'order'.
59 conjure call upon; as one would in exorcis-
ing an evil spirit.
60 at dinner The Courtesan has previously
dined with Antipholus E.

Or for my diamond the chain you promised,
And I'll be gone, sir, and not trouble you.
DROMIO S. Some devils ask but the parings of one's nail,
A rush, a hair, a drop of blood, a pin,
A nut, a cherry stone.   65
But she, more covetous, would have a chain.
Master, be wise; and if you give it her,
The devil will shake her chain, and fright us with it.
COURTESAN I pray you, sir, my ring, or else the chain.
I hope you do not mean to cheat me so.   70
ANTIPHOLUS S. Avaunt, thou witch! Come, Dromio, let us go.
DROMIO S. 'Fly pride', says the peacock. Mistress, that you know.
                          Exeunt Antipholus and Dromio
COURTESAN Now out of doubt Antipholus is mad,
Else would he never so demean himself.
A ring he hath of mine worth forty ducats,   75
And for the same he promised me a chain.
Both one and other he denies me now.
The reason that I gather he is mad,
Besides this present instance of his rage,
Is a mad tale he told today at dinner   80
Of his own doors being shut against his entrance.
Belike his wife, acquainted with his fits,
On purpose shut the doors against his way.
My way is now to hie home to his house,
And tell his wife that, being lunatic,   85

63–8] *As Capell (subst.); as prose* F   **72** SD] *Exit.* F

63–5 **parings ... stone** Possibly objects that
could be used in witchcraft.
67 and if if.
68 Compare Rev. 20.1–2: 'And I saw an angel
come down from heaven, having the key of the
bottomless pit, and a great chain in his hand. And
he took the dragon, that old serpent, which is the
Devil and Satan, and bound him a thousand
years.'
71 Avaunt Away with you. Such terms as
'witch' here, and 'Satan' (41), 'devil' (43), 'fiend'
(57), 'sorceress' (58), indicate Antipholus's
mounting terror.
72 Fly ... peacock The peacock is a traditional personification of pride. There is a pun on
'pride' in its meaning of sexual desire (*OED* sv *sb*
11, and compare Sonnet 144), and this

emphasises the irony of a peacock's bidding some
one to eschew pride, and Dromio's belief that the
Courtesan, an agent of the devil, is cheating
them.
74 demean himself conduct himself.
79 rage madness. This and 'mad' (73, 78, 80)
and 'lunatic' (85) reiterate the theme in the play
of madness applied in various forms to various
persons.
82 Belike Presumably.
83 way entrance.
84 hie home hasten directly.
84–8 There are few falsehoods, as distinct
from misunderstandings, in the play, but here the
Courtesan thinks up a lie to provide a 'rational'
explanation for confusions she does not understand, and to save her forty ducats.

He rushed into my house and took perforce
My ring away. This course I fittest choose,
For forty ducats is too much to lose.   *Exit*

4.4 *Enter* ANTIPHOLUS OF EPHESUS *with [the]* JAILER

ANTIPHOLUS E. Fear me not, man. I will not break away.
　　　　I'll give thee ere I leave thee so much money
　　　　To warrant thee as I am 'rested for.
　　　　My wife is in a wayward mood today,
　　　　And will not lightly trust the messenger   5
　　　　That I should be attached in Ephesus.
　　　　I tell you, 'twill sound harshly in her ears.

　　　　　　　Enter DROMIO OF EPHESUS, *with a rope's end*

　　　　Here comes my man. I think he brings the money.
　　　　How now, sir, have you that I sent you for?
DROMIO E. Here's that, I warrant you, will pay them all.   10
ANTIPHOLUS E. But where's the money?
DROMIO E. Why, sir, I gave the money for the rope.
ANTIPHOLUS E. Five hundred ducats, villain, for a rope?
DROMIO E. I'll serve you, sir, five hundred at the rate.
ANTIPHOLUS E. To what end did I bid thee hie thee home?   15
DROMIO E. To a rope's end, sir, and to that end am I returned.
ANTIPHOLUS E. And to that end, sir, I will welcome you.
　　　　　　　　　[He beats Dromio]
JAILER Good sir, be patient.
DROMIO E. Nay, 'tis for me to be patient. I am in adversity.

---

88 SD *Exit] Not in* F   **Act 4, Scene 4   4.4]** *Capell (subst.); not in* F   **0** SD OF EPHESUS] *Ephes.* F   **17** SD *He beats Dromio] Pope; not in* F

86 perforce by force.

Act 4, Scene 4
4.4 In this scene the confusions lead to downright violence and ugliness of temper.
　0 SD JAILER Presumably the Officer of 4.1.
　3 warrant thee assure your security (*OED* sv *v* 8).
　4 wayward perverse.
　5–6 will . . . attached will not readily believe a messenger who reports that I should be arrested. The run of the sense and of the rhythm suggests, I think, the omission of F comma at the end of 5.

9, 10 that that which.
　10 pay them all pay them all out (with a thrashing); compare 4.1.15–20.
　14 I'll supply you with five hundred (ropes) at that price, sir.
　16 to that end (1) to that beating; (2) for that purpose.
　19 patient . . . adversity Compare Ps. 94.13: 'That thou mayest give him patience in the time of adversity'.

JAILER Good now, hold thy tongue.   20
DROMIO E. Nay, rather persuade him to hold his hands.
ANTIPHOLUS E. Thou whoreson, senseless villain.
DROMIO E. I would I were senseless, sir, that I might not feel your
   blows.
ANTIPHOLUS E. Thou art sensible in nothing but blows; and so is an   25
   ass.
DROMIO E. I am an ass indeed. You may prove it by my long ears. I have
   served him from the hour of my nativity to this instant, and have
   nothing at his hands for my service but blows. When I am cold, he
   heats me with beating; when I am warm, he cools me with beating; I   30
   am waked with it when I sleep, raised with it when I sit, driven out of
   doors with it when I go from home, welcomed home with it when I
   return; nay, I bear it on my shoulders, as a beggar wont her brat, and
   I think when he hath lamed me I shall beg with it from door to door.

   Enter ADRIANA, LUCIANA, *the* COURTESAN,
   and a Schoolmaster called PINCH

ANTIPHOLUS E. Come, go along; my wife is coming yonder.   35
DROMIO E. Mistress, *respice finem* – 'respect your end', or rather, to
   prophesy like the parrot, 'Beware the rope's end.'
ANTIPHOLUS E. Wilt thou still talk?
                    [*He*] *beats Dromio*
COURTESAN How say you now? Is not your husband mad?
ADRIANA His incivility confirms no less.   40
   Good Doctor Pinch, you are a conjurer.
   Establish him in his true sense again,
   And I will please you what you will demand.
LUCIANA Alas, how fiery and how sharp he looks!
COURTESAN Mark how he trembles in his ecstasy.   45

20 Good now Now please; in a tone of
entreaty.

25 sensible ... blows responsive to nothing
but blows. A pun on 'sensible' – both in understanding and in feeling.

27–34 In its rhythms and its repetitions this
prose passage recalls Dromio's verse-idiom as it
is shown in such passages as 1.2.43–52 and
2.1.58–66. Other passages might be cited. See
pp. 15, 18 above.

27 long ears A pun on 'years', as in the
modern 'for donkey's years'.

33 wont is accustomed to do.

34 SD PINCH See 5.1.238–42 for a fuller description. He is called a 'schoolmaster' in F, and
'Doctor' a few lines lower – that is, a learned man
capable of being a 'conjurer' (41) because he
knows Latin, the language in which spirits may be
exorcised. Compare *Ham.* 1.1.42: 'Thou art a
scholar; speak to it.'

36 respice finem (1) think upon your end; (2)
think of a rope (*funem*) – i.e. an end by hanging.

38 still always, continually; as is normal in
Shakespeare.

45 ecstasy frenzy; often the state in which a
man's soul gave way to evil spirits.

PINCH Give me your hand, and let me feel your pulse.
ANTIPHOLUS E. There is my hand, and let it feel your ear.
                        [*He strikes Pinch*]
PINCH I charge thee, Satan, housed within this man,
          To yield possession to my holy prayers.
          And to thy state of darkness hie thee straight.   50
          I conjure thee by all the saints in heaven.
ANTIPHOLUS E. Peace, doting wizard, peace. I am not mad.
ADRIANA O that thou wert not, poor distressèd soul!
ANTIPHOLUS E. You, minion, you, are these your customers?
          Did this companion with the saffron face   55
          Revel and feast it at my house today,
          Whilst upon me the guilty doors were shut,
          And I denied to enter in my house?
ADRIANA O, husband, God doth know you dined at home,
          Where would you had remained until this time,   60
          Free from these slanders and this open shame.
ANTIPHOLUS E. Dined at home? [*To Dromio*] Thou, villain, what sayst
          thou?
DROMIO E. Sir, sooth to say, you did not dine at home.
ANTIPHOLUS E. Were not my doors locked up, and I shut out?
DROMIO E. Perdie, your doors were locked, and you shut out.   65
ANTIPHOLUS E. And did not she herself revile me there?
DROMIO E. Sans fable, she herself reviled you there.
ANTIPHOLUS E. Did not her kitchen-maid rail, taunt, and scorn me?
DROMIO E. Certes she did. The kitchen vestal scorned you.
ANTIPHOLUS E. And did not I in rage depart from thence?
DROMIO E. In verity you did. My bones bears witness,   70
          That since have felt the vigour of his rage.
ADRIANA Is't good to soothe him in these contraries?
PINCH It is no shame. The fellow finds his vein,
          And yielding to him humours well his frenzy.   75
ANTIPHOLUS E. Thou has suborned the goldsmith to arrest me.

47 SD *He strikes Pinch*] *Dyce; not in* F   62 Dined] F; Din'd I *Theobald;* I din'd *Capell*   62 SD *To Dromio*] *Foakes; not in* F

50 **straight** forthwith.

54 **minion** Normally = 'favourite', but could be a sexual partner of either sex; here the sense 'prostitute' is implied by 'customers' and 'companions' (used for disreputable company).

55 **saffron face** face resembling saffron in its orange-yellow colour.

61 **slanders** disgraceful imputations.

65 **Perdie** Indeed, By God (French *pardieu*).

69 **vestal** A reference to her function being like that of the vestal virgins, to keep the fire burning; of course ironical.

73 **soothe** humour.

73 **contraries** falsehoods.

74 **fellow** Dromio.

74 **finds his vein** understands his master's frame of mind. Pinch believes that Dromio is merely humouring his master in his madness.

ADRIANA Alas, I sent you money to redeem you,
    By Dromio here, who came in haste for it.
DROMIO E. Money by me? Heart and good will you might,
    But surely, master, not a rag of money.   80
ANTIPHOLUS E. Went'st not thou to her for a purse of ducats?
ADRIANA He came to me, and I delivered it.
LUCIANA And I am witness with her that she did.
DROMIO E. God and the ropemaker bear me witness
    That I was sent for nothing but a rope.   85
PINCH Mistress, both man and master is possessed;
    I know it by their pale and deadly looks.
    They must be bound and laid in some dark room.
ANTIPHOLUS E. [*To Adriana*] Say, wherefore didst thou lock me forth
    today,
    [*To Dromio*] And why dost thou deny the bag of gold?   90
ADRIANA I did not, gentle husband, lock thee forth.
DROMIO E. And, gentle master, I received no gold.
    But I confess, sir, that we were locked out.
ADRIANA Dissembling villain, thou speak'st false in both.
ANTIPHOLUS E. Dissembling harlot, thou art false in all,   95
    And art confederate with a damnèd pack
    To make a loathsome abject scorn of me.
    But with these nails I'll pluck out these false eyes
    That would behold in me this shameful sport.
ADRIANA O, bind him, bind him, let him not come near me!   100

Enter three or four and offer to bind him. He strives

PINCH More company! The fiend is strong within him.
LUCIANA Ay me, poor man, how pale and wan he looks.
ANTIPHOLUS E. What, will you murder me? Thou, jailer, thou,
    I am thy prisoner; wilt thou suffer them
      To make a rescue?
JAILER   Masters, let him go.   105

103 me? Thou, jailer, thou,] *Rowe*; me, thou Iailer thou? F   104–6] *As verse, Pope; as prose,* F

77 **redeem you** ransom you, buy your
freedom.
80 **rag of money** A semi-proverbial term for a
farthing. For discussion of 79–80 in relation to
the dating of the play see p. 2 above.
86 **both ... possessed** Pinch believes that
both are possessed by evil spirits.
88 **bound ... room** Compare *TN* 4.2, where
Malvolio is so confined.

100 SD As Wells observes, 'The imprecision
(*three or four*) suggests that it was written by
Shakespeare, not the stage manager, who would
need to know exactly how many attendants should
enter.'
105 **make a rescue** save someone by force
from legal custody.

He is my prisoner, and you shall not have him.

PINCH Go bind his man, for he is frantic too.

[Dromio is bound]

ADRIANA What wilt thou do, thou peevish officer?
Hast thou delight to see a wretched man
Do outrage and displeasure to himself? 110

JAILER He is my prisoner. If I let him go,
The debt he owes will be required of me.

ADRIANA I will discharge thee ere I go from thee.
Bear me forthwith unto his creditor,
And, knowing how the debt grows, I will pay it. 115
Good Master Doctor, see him safe conveyed
Home to my house. O most unhappy day!

ANTIPHOLUS E. O most unhappy strumpet!

DROMIO E. Master, I am here entered in bond for you.

ANTIPHOLUS E. Out on thee, villain! Wherefore dost thou mad me? 120

DROMIO E. Will you be bound for nothing? Be mad, good master; cry
'the devil!'

LUCIANA God help, poor souls, how idly do they talk!

ADRIANA Go bear him hence. Sister, go you with me.
Exeunt, [other than the] Jailer, Adriana, Luciana, and the Courtesan
Say now, whose suit is he arrested at? 125

JAILER One Angelo, a goldsmith. Do you know him?

ADRIANA I know the man. What is the sum he owes?

JAILER Two hundred ducats.

ADRIANA   Say, how grows it due?

JAILER Due for a chain your husband had of him.

ADRIANA He did bespeak a chain for me, but had it not.

COURTESAN Whenas your husband all in rage today 130
Came to my house and took away my ring,
The ring I saw upon his finger now,
Straight after did I meet him with a chain.

ADRIANA It may be so, but I did never see it. 135
Come, jailer, bring me where the goldsmith is.
I long to know the truth hereof at large.

---

123 help, poor] *Theobald;* help poore F   137 SD] *Enter Antipholus Siracusia with his Rapier drawne, and Dromio Sirac* F

108 **peevish** silly, spiteful.
110 **displeasure** injury.
113 **discharge** clear the debt.
115 **knowing . . . grows** when I know how the debt has arisen.

119 **in bond** (1) tied up; (2) pledged.
121–2 **cry 'the devil'** (1) relieve your anger by calling on the devil; (2) call on the devil presumed to be within you.
137 **at large** in full detail.

Enter ANTIPHOLUS [OF SYRACUSE] *and* DROMIO [OF
   SYRACUSE], *with their rapiers drawn*

LUCIANA God, for thy mercy, they are loose again!
ADRIANA And come with naked swords. Let's call more help
   To have them bound again.
JAILER   Away, they'll kill us!   140
               Exeunt omnes [apart from Antipholus S. and Dromio S.],
                              as fast as may be, frighted
ANTIPHOLUS S. I see these witches are afraid of swords.
DROMIO S. She that would be your wife now ran from you.
ANTIPHOLUS S. Come to the Centaur. Fetch our stuff from thence.
   I long that we were safe and sound aboard.
DROMIO S. Faith, stay here this night. They will surely do us no harm.   145
   You saw they speak us fair, give us gold. Methinks they are such a
   gentle nation that, but for the mountain of mad flesh that claims
   marriage of me, I could find it in my heart to stay here still, and turn
   witch.
ANTIPHOLUS S. I will not stay tonight for all the town;   150
   Therefore away, to get our stuff aboard.
                                                            Exeunt

5.1 *Enter [the* SECOND] MERCHANT *and [*ANGELO] *the goldsmith*

ANGELO I am sorry, sir, that I have hindered you,
   But I protest he had the chain of me,
   Though most dishonestly he doth deny it.
2 MERCHANT How is the man esteemed here in the city?
ANGELO Of very reverend reputation, sir;   5
   Of credit infinite, highly beloved,
   Second to none that lives here in the city.

139–40] swords. Let's ... help / ... again. *(Run all out.)* Away, they'll kill us. *Hanmer;* swords, / Let's call more
helpe to haue them bound againe. / *Runne all out.* / *Off.* Away, they'l kill vs. / *Exeunt omnes, as fast as may be, frighted.*
F   146 saw ... speak ... give] F; saw ... spake ... gave *Rowe*   Act 5, Scene 1   5.1] *Actus Quintus. Scæna Prima.*
F   0 SD] *Enter the Merchant and the Goldsmith.* F   4 SH 2MERCHANT] *Mar.* F *(so throughout scene)*

142 **would be your wife** claimed to be your   Act 5, Scene 1
wife.   1 **hindered** See 4.1.1–6.
   143, 151 **stuff** belongings.   5 **reverend** A necessary emendation of F
                                                 'reverent'.

His word might bear my wealth at any time.

2 MERCHANT Speak softly. Yonder, as I think, he walks.

Enter ANTIPHOLUS [OF SYRACUSE] *and* DROMIO
[OF SYRACUSE] *again*

ANGELO 'Tis so; and that self chain about his neck   10
Which he forswore most monstrously to have.
Good sir, draw near to me; I'll speak to him.
Signior Antipholus, I wonder much
That you would put me to this shame and trouble,
And not without some scandal to yourself,   15
With circumstance and oaths so to deny
This chain, which now you wear so openly.
Beside the charge, the shame, imprisonment,
You have done wrong to this my honest friend,
Who, but for staying on our controversy,   20
Had hoisted sail and put to sea today.
This chain you had of me. Can you deny it?

ANTIPHOLUS S. I think I had. I never did deny it.

2 MERCHANT Yes, that you did, sir, and forswore it, too.

ANTIPHOLUS S. Who heard me to deny it or forswear it?   25

2 MERCHANT These ears of mine, thou know'st, did hear thee.
Fie on thee, wretch. 'Tis pity that thou liv'st
To walk where any honest men resort.

ANTIPHOLUS S. Thou art a villain to impeach me thus.
I'll prove mine honour and mine honesty   30
Against thee presently, if thou dar'st stand.

8 He could borrow all my wealth at any time on the strength of his mere word.

9 SD The two Syracusans were on the stage at the end of the preceding scene, only nine lines earlier, and in effect the action carries straight on. Was it felt necessary to break the action for a few moments to bring Angelo on to the stage to confront Antipholus? Or could he and the Merchant have appeared from the side and spoken 'apart'? Of course we do not know who made the act-divisions.

10 self same.

12 to me Angelo presumably wants the Merchant's close support.

16 circumstance close argument.

18 charge expense.

18 imprisonment The Merchant had caused Angelo to be imprisoned (4.1.69–71). How do they come to be walking together now as friends? However, this inconsistency, like others, would not be noticed in a performance.

20 but . . . controversy were it not that he was kept back by our dispute.

29 impeach accuse.

30 honesty The word can carry its modern sense, but it can also be a synonym for 'honour', as so often in *Oth*. Probably both senses are implied here, reinforcing 'honour' in the same line.

31 presently immediately; the normal Shakespearean sense, as at 3.2.131 and 4.1.32.

31 stand put it to the test.

2 MERCHANT I dare, and do defy thee for a villain.

They draw

Enter ADRIANA, LUCIANA, *the* COURTESAN, *and others*

ADRIANA Hold, hurt him not, for God's sake; he is mad.
    Some get within him, take his sword away.
    Bind Dromio too, and bear them to my house.   35
DROMIO S. Run, master, run! For God's sake take a house.
    This is some priory. In, or we are spoiled.

Exeunt [Antipholus of Syracuse and Dromio of Syracuse]
to the priory

Enter [ÆMILIA, the] Lady Abbess

ABBESS Be quiet, people. Wherefore throng you hither?
ADRIANA To fetch my poor distracted husband hence.
    Let us come in, that we may bind him fast   40
    And bear him home for his recovery.
ANGELO I knew he was not in his perfect wits.
2 MERCHANT I am sorry now that I did draw on him.
ABBESS How long hath this possession held the man?
ADRIANA This week he hath been heavy, sour, sad,   45
    And much, much different from the man he was.
    But till this afternoon his passion
    Ne'er brake into extremity of rage.
ABBESS Hath he not lost much wealth by wrack of sea?
    Buried some dear friend? Hath not else his eye   50
    Strayed his affection in unlawful love –
    A sin prevailing much in youthful men,
    Who give their eyes the liberty of gazing?
    Which of these sorrows is he subject to?
ADRIANA To none of these except it be the last,   55

33 God's] F3; God F   37 SD *Antipholus of Syracuse and Dromio of Syracuse*] *Not in* F   37 SD.3 *ÆMILIA, the*] *Not in* F

32 SD **They draw** This seems to refer only to Antipholus and the Merchant (not Angelo), who later refers twice to having drawn his sword on Antipholus (43, 263); Angelo never mentions having done so. The direction '*and others*' is vague, like '*three or four*' at 4.4.100.
34 **within him** within his guard.
36 **take** take to, go into.
37 **spoiled** undone, ruined.
38 With the entry of the Abbess violence is brought to an end and order begins to be

restored. She is the *dea ex machina*, providing, as Foakes observes, a 'hint of a providential solution of difficulties'.
44 **possession** i.e. by evil spirits, or madness; compare 4.4.49.
45 **This week** All this week. 'Sad' = melancholy.
47 **passion** affliction, disorder.
48 **rage** madness; as at 4.3.79, and elsewhere.
49 **wrack of sea** shipwreck.
51 **Strayed** Led astray.

Namely some love that drew him oft from home.
ABBESS You should for that have reprehended him.
ADRIANA Why, so I did.
ABBESS   Ay, but not rough enough.
ADRIANA As roughly as my modesty would let me.
ABBESS Haply in private.
ADRIANA   And in assemblies, too.   60
ABBESS Ay, but not enough.
ADRIANA It was the copy of our conference.
In bed he slept not for my urging it;
At board he fed not for my urging it.
Alone, it was the subject of my theme;   65
In company I often glanced at it.
Still did I tell him it was vile and bad.
ABBESS And thereof came it that the man was mad.
The venom clamours of a jealous woman
Poisons more deadly than a mad dog's tooth.   70
It seems his sleeps were hindered by thy railing,
And thereof comes it that his head is light.
Thou sayst his meat was sauced with thy upbraidings;
Unquiet meals make ill digestions.
Thereof the raging fire of fever bred;   75
And what's a fever but a fit of madness?
Thou sayst his sports were hindered by thy brawls;
Sweet recreation barred, what doth ensue
But moody and dull melancholy,
Kinsman to grim and comfortless despair,   80
And at her heels a huge infectious troop
Of pale distemperatures and foes to life?
In food, in sport, and life-preserving rest
To be disturbed would mad or man or beast.

66 glanced at] *Pope;* glanced F

62 **copy** theme; a formal rhetorical term (*copia verborum*) which gives 'conference' a formal effect too, as though their conversation were a formal disputation.
62 **conference** conversation.
66 **glanced at** alluded to; 'at' is not in F, but seems to be required for both sense and metre; the combination appears at *MND* 2.1.75 and *JC* 1.2.317.
67 **Still** Continually.
67–8 'Adriana falls into the Abbess's trap, and

the rhyme here marks its closure' (Foakes).
69 **venom** Here as an adjective; the plural 'clamours' is followed by the singular 'poisons' – a common usage in Shakespeare.
77 **sports** pastimes.
79 The line is metrically defective, but effective as it stands.
80 **Kinsman** A word that can denote almost any relationship.
82 **distemperatures** disorders, ailments.

  The consequence is, then, thy jealous fits   85
  Hath scared thy husband from the use of wits.
LUCIANA She never reprehended him but mildly,
  When he demeaned himself rough, rude, and wildly.
  [*To Adriana*] Why bear you these rebukes, and answer not?
ADRIANA She did betray me to my own reproof.   90
  Good people, enter, and lay hold on him.
ABBESS No, not a creature enters in my house.
ADRIANA Then let your servants bring my husband forth.
ABBESS Neither. He took this place for sanctuary,
  And it shall privilege him from your hands   95
  Till I have brought him to his wits again,
  Or lose my labour in assaying it.
ADRIANA I will attend my husband, be his nurse,
  Diet his sickness, for it is my office,
  And will have no attorney but myself.   100
  And therefore let me have him home with me.
ABBESS Be patient, for I will not let him stir
  Till I have used the approvèd means I have,
  With wholesome syrups, drugs, and holy prayers,
  To make of him a formal man again.   105
  It is a branch and parcel of mine oath,
  A charitable duty of my order.
  Therefore depart, and leave him here with me.
ADRIANA I will not hence and leave my husband here.
  And ill it doth beseem your holiness   110
  To separate the husband and the wife.
ABBESS Be quiet, and depart. Thou shalt not have him. [*Exit*]
LUCIANA [*To Adriana*] Complain unto the Duke of this indignity.
ADRIANA Come, go. I will fall prostrate at his feet,
  And never rise until my tears and prayers   115
  Have won his grace to come in person hither
  And take perforce my husband from the Abbess.

112 SD *Exit*] Theobald; *not in* F

86 **Hath** A singular verb with a plural subject.
88 **demeaned himself** conducted himself; compare 4.3.74.
90 **betray . . . reproof** 'trick me into recognizing my own faults' (Wells).
98–9 Noble suggests (p. 109) that this may be an echo of the phrases in the marriage service

(Book of Common Prayer), 'to have and to hold . . . in sickness and in health'.
100 **attorney** substitute to act on my behalf.
103 **approvèd** tried, tested.
105 **formal** normal, sane.
106 **parcel** essential part.

2 MERCHANT By this, I think, the dial points at five.
　　　　Anon, I'm sure, the Duke himself in person
　　　　Comes this way to the melancholy vale,   120
　　　　The place of death and sorry execution
　　　　Behind the ditches of the abbey here.
ANGELO Upon what cause?
2 MERCHANT To see a reverend Syracusian merchant,
　　　　Who put unluckily into this bay   125
　　　　Against the laws and statutes of this town,
　　　　Beheaded publicly for his offence.
ANGELO See where they come. We will behold his death.
LUCIANA Kneel to the Duke before he pass the abbey.

Enter [SOLINUS,] *the Duke of Ephesus, and* [EGEON,] *the Merchant of
Syracuse, barehead, with the* HEADSMAN, *and other officers*

DUKE Yet once again proclaim it publicly.   130
　　　　If any friend will pay the sum for him,
　　　　He shall not die, so much we tender him.
ADRIANA Justice, most sacred Duke, against the Abbess!
DUKE She is a virtuous and a reverend lady.
　　　　It cannot be that she hath done thee wrong.   135
ADRIANA May it please your grace, Antipholus my husband,
　　　　Who I made lord of me and all I had
　　　　At your important letters – this ill day
　　　　A most outrageous fit of madness took him,
　　　　That desperately he hurried through the street,   140
　　　　With him his bondman all as mad as he,
　　　　Doing displeasure to the citizens
　　　　By rushing in their houses, bearing thence
　　　　Rings, jewels, anything his rage did like.

121 death] F3; depth F　　129 SD SOLINUS] *Not in* F　　129 SD EGEON] *Not in* F

118 **By this** 'By this time' is the usual inter-
pretation. However, Mr Walter Hodges has suggested to me, very plausibly, that the words indicate the ringing of the priory bell, included in his
conjectural stage setting in illustration 7 (p. 26
above).

118 **five** The time normally arranged for the
settling of business affairs (see 1.2.26 and 4.1.10)
now emerges as the hour also appointed for
Egeon's execution.

119 **Anon** Shortly.

120 **melancholy vale** Just possibly a topical
reference to Finsbury Fields. See T. W. Bald-

win's *William Shakspere Adapts a Hanging* (1931).

121 **sorry** sorrowful.

129 SD Egeon is '*barehead*', ready for execution,
and 'bound' (294). Presumably the Headsman
would be recognised by his costume and his axe.

137 **Who** A not infrequent usage in
Shakespeare (see Abbott 274). It is emended to
'whom' in F2.

138 **important** importunate, urgent.

140 **That** With the result that.

140 **desperately** violently, recklessly.

142 **displeasure** annoyance, harm.

Once did I get him bound, and sent him home   145
Whilst to take order for the wrongs I went,
That here and there his fury had committed.
Anon, I wot not by what strong escape,
He broke from those that had the guard of him,
And with his mad attendant and himself,   150
Each one with ireful passion, with drawn swords
Met us again, and, madly bent on us,
Chased us away; till, raising of more aid,
We came again to bind them. Then they fled
Into this abbey, whither we pursued them;   155
And here the Abbess shuts the gates on us,
And will not suffer us to fetch him out,
Nor send him forth that we may bear him hence.
Therefore, most gracious Duke, with thy command
Let him be brought forth, and borne hence for help.   160
DUKE Long since thy husband served me in my wars,
And I to thee engaged a prince's word,
When thou didst make him master of thy bed,
To do him all the grace and good I could.
Go, some of you, knock at the abbey gate,   165
And bid the Lady Abbess come to me.
I will determine this before I stir.

Enter a MESSENGER

MESSENGER O mistress, mistress, shift and save yourself!
My master and his man are both broke loose,
Beaten the maids a-row, and bound the Doctor,   170
Whose beard they have singed off with brands of fire,
And ever as it blazed they threw on him
Great pails of puddled mire to quench the hair.
My master preaches patience to him, and the while

155 whither] F (whether)

146 **take order for** make arrangements about.
148 **strong escape** escape by violent means.
152 **bent** turned.
153 **raising of** Abbott notes (178) that a (to us
redundant) 'of' is common after participles.
160 **help** treatment, relief.
167 **determine** settle.
168 **shift** make off. The speech heading
MESSENGER does not appear in F. The Messen-

ger's confused syntax reflects the breathless haste
with which he gives his news.
170 **a-row** one after another.
171–3 Commentators have drawn attention to
resemblances to Marlowe's *Edward II* (5.3), in
which the King, standing in 'mire and puddle',
has his beard forcibly shaved by Matrevis and
Gurney. See above, p. 2.
173 **puddled** stirred up.

His man with scissors nicks him like a fool;   175
And sure, unless you send some present help,
Between them they will kill the conjurer.

ADRIANA Peace, fool; thy master and his man are here,
And that is false thou dost report to us.

MESSENGER Mistress, upon my life I tell you true.   180
I have not breathed almost since I did see it.
He cries for you, and vows, if he can take you,
To scorch your face and to disfigure you.
                      Cry within
Hark, hark, I hear him, mistress. Fly, be gone!

DUKE Come, stand by me. Fear nothing. Guard with halberds!   185

ADRIANA Ay me, it is my husband. Witness you
That he is borne about invisible.
Even now we housed him in the abbey here,
And now he's there, past thought of human reason.

Enter ANTIPHOLUS OF EPHESUS *and* DROMIO OF EPHESUS

ANTIPHOLUS E. Justice, most gracious Duke, O grant me justice,   190
Even for the service that long since I did thee
When I bestrid thee in the wars, and took
Deep scars to save thy life. Even for the blood
That then I lost for thee, now grant me justice.

EGEON [*Aside*] Unless the fear of death doth make me dote,   195
I see my son Antipholus, and Dromio.

ANTIPHOLUS E. Justice, sweet prince, against that woman there,
She whom thou gav'st to me to be my wife;
That hath abusèd and dishonoured me
Even in the strength and height of injury.   200
Beyond imagination is the wrong
That she this day hath shameless thrown on me.

---

175 **like a fool** Professional fools traditionally shaved their hair and beards, or were tonsured, like monks.

177 **conjurer** At 4.4.41 Pinch is described as a conjurer, although he is first introduced as a schoolmaster.

183 **scorch** As Pinch's beard was scorched with 'brands of fire' (171); but very probably also a pun on scorched (= scored) – compare *Mac.* 3.3.13: 'We have scorched the snake.'

185 **halberds** Presumably some of the officers

referred to in 129 SD are carrying halberds, spears fitted with axe-heads.

187–9 How could Adriana not now be convinced that things 'past thought of human reason', supernatural influences, are at work in Ephesus?

192 **bestrid** stood over.

195–6 Printed as prose in F, perhaps, as Foakes observes, because there was no space to print 'dote' in 195; 'dote' = 'lose my wits', the result of old age (as in 'dotage').

200 In the most injurious manner conceivable.

DUKE Discover how, and thou shalt find me just.

ANTIPHOLUS E. This day, great Duke, she shut the doors upon me
     While she with harlots feasted in my house.   205

DUKE A grievous fault. Say, woman, didst thou so?

ADRIANA No, my good lord. Myself, he, and my sister
     Today did dine together. So befall my soul,
     As this is false he burdens me withal.

LUCIANA Ne'er may I look on day nor sleep on night   210
     But she tells to your highness simple truth.

ANGELO [*Aside*] O perjured woman! They are both forsworn;
     In this the madman justly chargeth them.

ANTIPHOLUS E. My liege, I am advisèd what I say,
     Neither disturbed with the effect of wine   215
     Nor heady-rash provoked with raging ire,
     Albeit my wrongs might make one wiser mad.
     This woman locked me out this day from dinner.
     That goldsmith there, were he not packed with her,
     Could witness it, for he was with me then,   220
     Who parted with me to go fetch a chain,
     Promising to bring it to the Porpentine,
     Where Balthasar and I did dine together.
     Our dinner done, and he not coming thither,
     I went to seek him. In the street I met him,   225
     And in his company that gentleman.
     There did this perjured goldsmith swear me down
     That I this day of him received the chain,
     Which, God he knows, I saw not. For the which
     He did arrest me with an officer.   230
     I did obey, and sent my peasant home
     For certain ducats. He with none returned.
     Then fairly I bespoke the officer

---

212 SD *Aside*] *Not in* F

203 **Discover** Reveal.

205 **harlots** Though more commonly applied to women of loose life, the word originally meant a rogue or low fellow, and could be applied to men, in both cases with less strong connotations than today.

208 **So ... soul** May the fate of my soul depend on it.

209 **burdens me withal** charges me with.

214 **advisèd** aware of.

216 Nor provoked to impetuous rashness by raging fury.

219 **packed with** in league with.

221 **parted** departed.

226 **that gentleman** The Merchant.

227 **swear me down** swear in spite of my denial.

231 **peasant** A term meaning little more than 'servant'.

233 **bespoke** asked.

To go in person with me to my house.
By the way we met   235
My wife, her sister, and a rabble more
Of vile confederates. Along with them
They brought one Pinch, a hungry, lean-faced villain,
A mere anatomy, a mountebank,
A threadbare juggler and a fortune-teller,   240
A needy, hollow-eyed, sharp-looking wretch,
A living dead man. This pernicious slave,
Forsooth, took on him as a conjurer,
And gazing in mine eyes, feeling my pulse
And with no face, as 'twere, outfacing me,   245
Cries out I was possessed. Then all together
They fell upon me, bound me, bore me thence,
And in a dark and dankish vault at home
There left me and my man, both bound together,
Till, gnawing with my teeth my bonds in sunder,   250
I gained my freedom, and immediately
Ran hither to your grace, whom I beseech
To give me ample satisfaction
From these deep shames and great indignities.
ANGELO My lord, in truth, thus far I witness with him: 255
That he dined not at home, but was locked out.
DUKE But had he such a chain of thee, or no?
ANGELO He had, my lord, and when he ran in here
These people saw the chain about his neck.
2 MERCHANT *[To Antipholus]* Besides, I will be sworn these ears of
mine   260
Heard you confess you had the chain of him
After you first forswore it on the mart,
And thereupon I drew my sword on you;
And then you fled into this abbey here,
From whence I think you are come by miracle.   265
ANTIPHOLUS E. I never came within these abbey walls,
Nor ever didst thou draw thy sword on me.
I never saw the chain, so help me heaven,
And this is false you burden me withal.

235–6 By the way . . . more] *As Malone; one line in* F   246 all together] *Rowe;* altogether F

239 **anatomy** skeleton.   245 **And though** (being so scraggy) he has no
239 **mountebank** quack, charlatan.   face, as it were, staring me down.
240 **juggler** Closely related to 'sorcerer'.   246 **possessed** mad; see above, 44 n.

DUKE Why, what an intricate impeach is this!   270
    I think you all have drunk of Circe's cup.
    If here you housed him, here he would have been.
    If he were mad, he would not plead so coldly.
    [To Adriana] You say he dined at home. The goldsmith here
    Denies that saying. *[To Dromio]* Sirrah, what say you?   275
DROMIO E. Sir, he dined with her there, at the Porpentine.
COURTESAN He did, and from my finger snatched that ring.
ANTIPHOLUS E. 'Tis true, my liege, this ring I had of her.
DUKE Saw'st thou him enter at the abbey here?
COURTESAN As sure, my liege, as I do see your grace.   280
DUKE Why, this is strange. Go call the Abbess hither.
    I think you are all mated, or stark mad.
                                Exit one to the Abbess
EGEON Most mighty Duke, vouchsafe me speak a word.
    Haply I see a friend will save my life
    And pay the sum that may deliver me.   285
DUKE Speak freely, Syracusian, what thou wilt.
EGEON Is not your name, sir, called Antipholus?
    And is not that your bondman Dromio?
DROMIO E. Within this hour I was his bondman, sir,
    But he, I thank him, gnawed in two my cords.   290
    Now am I Dromio, and his man, unbound.
EGEON I am sure you both of you remember me.
DROMIO E. Ourselves we do remember, sir, by you,
    For lately we were bound as you are now.
    You are not Pinch's patient, are you, sir?   295
EGEON Why look you strange on me? You know me well.
ANTIPHOLUS E. I never saw you in my life till now.
EGEON O, grief hath changed me since you saw me last,
    And careful hours with time's deformèd hand
    Have written strange defeatures in my face.   300

283 SH EGEON] *Fa.* F *(Fa., Fat., Fath., / or / Father. / throughout scene)*

270 **impeach** accusation, charge.
271 **Circe's cup** The potion with which the sorceress Circe transformed men into swine (*Odyssey*, Bk x). Ovid also tells the story in his *Metamorphoses*. The transformation images of the play here reach their climax.
273 **coldly** coolly, rationally.
282 **mated** stupefied, bewildered. The Duke himself is stupefied by all the contradictions, and thus drawn into the theme of confusion.

288, 289 **bondman** Puns, continued in 'unbound' at 291.
299 **careful** full of care.
299 **deformèd** deforming. Foakes suggests that it may also refer to 'the withered hand of Father Time, as commonly personified and depicted', and compares 2.2.64–5.
300 **defeatures** disfigurements.

But tell me yet, dost thou not know my voice?

ANTIPHOLUS E. Neither.

EGEON Dromio, nor thou?

DROMIO E. No, trust me, sir, nor I.

EGEON   I am sure thou dost.

DROMIO E. Ay, sir, but I am sure I do not, and whatsoever a man   305
denies, you are now bound to believe him.

EGEON Not know my voice? O time's extremity,
Hast thou so cracked and splitted my poor tongue
In seven short years that here my only son
Knows not my feeble key of untuned cares?   310
Though now this grainèd face of mine be hid
In sap-consuming winter's drizzled snow,
And all the conduits of my blood froze up,
Yet hath my night of life some memory,
My wasting lamps some fading glimmer left,   315
My dull deaf ears a little use to hear.
All these old witnesses, I cannot err,
Tell me thou art my son Antipholus.

ANTIPHOLUS E. I never saw my father in my life.

EGEON But seven years since, in Syracusa, boy,   320
Thou know'st we parted. But perhaps, my son,
Thou sham'st to acknowledge me in misery.

ANTIPHOLUS E. The Duke and all that know me in the city
Can witness with me that it is not so.
I ne'er saw Syracusa in my life.   325

DUKE I tell thee, Syracusian, twenty years
Have I been patron to Antipholus,
During which time he ne'er saw Syracusa.

305–6] *As prose,* F; *as verse,* Capell

306 bound Another pun, since Egeon is actually bound; compare 288–91.

307 extremity extreme severity.

308 splitted For this form compare 1.1.103,
and *Ant.* 5.1.24: 'splitted the heart'.

309 seven . . . years At 1.1.132 it is five years.
The discrepancy is probably accidental, but in
any case would not be noticed in the theatre. At
400 the Abbess speaks of the thirty-three years
during which she was parted from her family.

310 my feeble . . . cares the feeble tone of my
voice, changed by grief; compare *Lear* 4.7.15,

'th'untuned and jarring senses', and *The Rape of
Lucrece* 1214, 'with untuned tongue'.

311 grainèd lined, furrowed (like the grain of
wood); compare *Cor.* 4.4.108: 'My grained ash'.

312 His beard, whitened as though by the snow
of winter, when the sap of plants is dormant.

313 conduits veins (channels); 'froze' for
'frozen' – compare 'arose' (388), which Abbott
(343) explains as a preterite used as a past
participle.

315 lamps eyes.

320 seven years Compare 309 n.

I see thy age and dangers make thee dote.

Enter [ÆMILIA,] *the Abbess, with* ANTIPHOLUS OF SYRACUSE *and*
DROMIO OF SYRACUSE

ABBESS Most mighty Duke, behold a man much wronged.   330
                        All gather to see them
ADRIANA I see two husbands, or mine eyes deceive me.
DUKE One of these men is genius to the other;
        And so, of these, which is the natural man,
        And which the spirit? Who deciphers them?
DROMIO S. I, sir, am Dromio. Command him away.   335
DROMIO E. I, sir, am Dromio. Pray let me stay.
ANTIPHOLUS S. Egeon, art thou not? or else his ghost.
DROMIO S. O, my old master! Who hath bound him here?
ABBESS Whoever bound him, I will loose his bonds,
        And gain a husband by his liberty.   340
        Speak, old Egeon, if thou be'st the man
        That hadst a wife once called Æmilia,
        That bore thee at a burden two fair sons.
        O, if thou be'st the same Egeon, speak,
        And speak unto the same Æmilia.   345
DUKE Why, here begins his morning story right.
        These two Antipholus', these two so like,
        And these two Dromios, one in semblance,
        Besides her urging of her wrack at sea –
        These are the parents to these children,   350
        Which accidentally are met together.
EGEON If I dream not, thou art Æmilia.
        If thou art she, tell me, where is that son
        That floated with thee on the fatal raft?
ABBESS By men of Epidamnum he and I   355

329 SD ÆMILIA] *Not in* F

329 SD A most effectively dramatic moment.
For the first time the pairs of twins are brought
together. No wonder that (330 SD) *All gather to see
them.*
332 **genius** The attendant spirit, which in
ancient times was believed to be allotted to a man;
it resembled him identically, and through his life
governed his fortunes. In F the word is italicised
as if it was foreign, but the notion was common
knowledge in Shakespeare's day; compare *JC*

2.1.66: 'The genius and the mortal instruments'.
334 **deciphers** distinguishes.
343 **at a burden** at a single birth; compare
1.1.50.
355–9 **By men … of Epidamnum** At
1.1.111 Egeon says that Æmilia was picked up by
'fishermen of Corinth'. The inconsistency is
immaterial, and would surely pass unnoticed on
the stage.

And the twin Dromio all were taken up;
But by and by rude fishermen of Corinth
By force took Dromio and my son from them,
And me they left with those of Epidamnum.
What then became of them I cannot tell;   360
I, to this fortune that you see me in.

DUKE [*To Antipholus of Syracuse*] Antipholus, thou cam'st from Corinth
    first.

ANTIPHOLUS S. No, sir, not I. I came from Syracuse.

DUKE Stay, stand apart. I know not which is which.

ANTIPHOLUS E. I came from Corinth, my most gracious lord.   365

DROMIO E. And I with him.

ANTIPHOLUS E. Brought to this town by that most famous warrior
    Duke Menaphon, your most renownèd uncle.

ADRIANA Which of you two did dine with me today?

ANTIPHOLUS S. I, gentle mistress.

ADRIANA   And are you not my husband?   370

ANTIPHOLUS E. No, I say nay to that.

ANTIPHOLUS S. And so do I. Yet did she call me so,
    And this fair gentlewoman, her sister here,
    Did call me brother. [*To Luciana*] What I told you then
    I hope I shall have leisure to make good,   375
    If this be not a dream I see and hear.

ANGELO That is the chain, sir, which you had of me.

ANTIPHOLUS S. I think it be, sir. I deny it not.

ANTIPHOLUS E. And you, sir, for this chain arrested me.

ANGELO I think I did, sir. I deny it not.   380

ADRIANA [*To Antipholus of Ephesus*] I sent you money, sir, to be your bail
    By Dromio, but I think he brought it not.

DROMIO E. No, none by me.

ANTIPHOLUS S. This purse of ducats I received from you,
    And Dromio my man did bring them me.   385
    I see we still did meet each other's man,
    And I was ta'en for him, and he for me,
    And thereupon these errors are arose.

374 SD *To Luciana*] *Not in* F

357 **rude** (1) rough; (2) simple.
368 Duke Menaphon Not mentioned elsewhere, nor does this matter. The name is used
also by Marlowe in *Tamburlaine*, and in Robert
Greene's romance *Menaphon*.

386 **still** continually, repeatedly.
388 **arose** See 'froze' (313) and n.

ANTIPHOLUS E. These ducats pawn I for my father here.
DUKE It shall not need. Thy father hath his life.   390
COURTESAN Sir, I must have that diamond from you.
ANTIPHOLUS E. There, take it, and much thanks for my good cheer.
ABBESS Renownèd Duke, vouchsafe to take the pains
        To go with us into the abbey here,
        And hear at large discoursèd all our fortunes,   395
        And all that are assembled in this place,
        That by this sympathisèd one day's error
        Have suffered wrong. Go, keep us company,
        And we shall make full satisfaction.
        Thirty-three years have I but gone in travail   400
        Of you, my sons, and till this present hour
        My heavy burden ne'er deliverèd.
        The Duke, my husband, and my children both,
        And you, the calendars of their nativity,
        Go to a gossips' feast, and go with me.   405
        After so long grief, such nativity.
DUKE With all my heart I'll gossip at this feast.
                            Exeunt omnes, [except] the two Dromios
                                and [the] two brothers [Antipholus]
DROMIO S. [*To Antipholus of Ephesus*] Master, shall I fetch your stuff
        from shipboard?
ANTIPHOLUS E. Dromio, what stuff of mine hast thou embarked?
DROMIO S. Your goods that lay at host, sir, in the Centaur.   410
ANTIPHOLUS S. He speaks to me; I am your master, Dromio.
        Come, go with us, we'll look to that anon.
        Embrace thy brother there, rejoice with him.
                            Exeunt [the brothers Antipholus]
DROMIO S. There is a fat friend at your master's house
        That kitchened me for you today at dinner.   415

402 burden ne'er] *Dyce;* burthen are F   407 SD] *Exeunt omnes. Manet the two Dromio's and two Brothers.* F   413 SD
Exeunt the brothers Antipholus] Exit F

391 **diamond** Her ring (see 4.3.61).
397 **sympathisèd** shared in.
400 **Thirty-three years** Theobald added the eighteen years of 1.1.125 to the 'seven years' of 320 above, and emended to 'Twenty-five'. At 1.1.132 Egeon says that he has been searching for 'five summers'. The audience would hardly notice this further inconsistency.

404 **calendars ... nativity** The Dromios, who represent the age of the Antipholuses. Compare 1.2.41.
405 **gossips' feast** A feast of godparents at a baptism at which each of the main characters is to be symbolically re-baptised, and discover, or rediscover, his identity.
410 **at host** at the inn; compare 'hostel'.
412 **anon** soon, shortly.
415 **kitchened** entertained in the kitchen.

> She now shall be my sister, not my wife.

DROMIO E. Methinks you are my glass, and not my brother.
> I see by you I am a sweet-faced youth.
> Will you walk in to see their gossiping?

DROMIO S. Not I, sir. You are my elder.   420

DROMIO E. That's a question. How shall we try it?

DROMIO S. We'll draw cuts for the senior. Till then, lead thou first.

DROMIO E. Nay then, thus:
> We came into the world like brother and brother,
> And now let's go hand in hand, not one before another.   425

Exeunt

417 **glass** mirror.
422 **draw cuts** draw lots (here presumably
straws cut into different lengths).

APPENDIX 1: THE PERFORMANCE OF 1594

From the *Gesta Grayorum*, ed. W. W. Greg (Malone Society Reprints), 1914, pp. 22–4; by permission of the Malone Society

The next grand Night was intended to be upon *Innocents-Day* at Night; at which time there was a great Presence of Lords, Ladies, and worshipful Personages, that did expect some notable Performance at that time; which, indeed, had been effected, if the multitude of Beholders had not been so exceeding great, that thereby there was no convenient room for those that were Actors; by reason whereof, very good Inventions and Conceipts could not have opportunity to be applauded, which otherwise would have been great Contentation to the Beholders. Against which time, our Friend, the *Inner Temple*, determined to send their Ambassador to our Prince.

. . . When the Ambassador was placed . . . and that there was something to be performed for the Delight of the Beholders, there arose such a disordered Tumult and Crowd upon the Stage, that there was no Opportunity to effect that which was intended . . . The Lord Ambassador . . . would not stay longer at that time . . . After their Departure the Throngs and Tumult did somewhat cease, although so much of them continued, as was able to disorder and confound any good intention whatsoever. In regard whereof, as also for that the Sports intended were especially for the gracing of the *Templarians*, it was thought good not to offer any thing of Account, saving Dancing and Revelling with Gentlewomen; and after such sports, a Comedy of Errors (like to *Plautus* his *Menechmus*) was played by the Players. So that Night was begun, and continued to the end, in nothing but Confusion and Errors, whereupon, it was ever afterwards called, *The Night of Errors*.

. . . The next Night upon this Occasion, we preferred Judgments thick and threefold, which were read publickly by the Clerk of the Crown, being all against a Sorcerer or Conjurer that was supposed to be the Cause of that confused Inconvenience.[1] Therein was contained, How he had caused the Stage to be built, and Scaffolds to be reared to the top of the House, to increase Expectation . . . Also that he caused Throngs and Tumults, Crowds and Outrages, to disturb our whole Proceedings. And Lastly, that he had foisted a Company of base and common Fellows, to make up our Disorders with a Play of Errors and Confusions; and that that Night had gained to us Discredit, and it self a Nickname of Errors . . . The Prisoner appealed to the Prince his Excellency for Justice . . . The Prince gave leave to the Master of the Requests that he should read the Petition; wherein was a Disclosure of all the Knavery and Juggling of the Attorney and Sollicitor, which had brought all this Law-stuff on purpose to blind the Eyes of his Excellency, and all the honourable Court there, going about to make them think, that those things, which they all saw and perceived sensibly to be in very deed done, and actually performed, were

---

[1] Is this perhaps an echo of Dr Pinch?

nothing else but vain Illusions, Fancies, Dreams and Enchantments, and to be wrought and compassed by the Means of a poor harmless Wretch, that never heard of such great Matters in all his life . . . The Prisoner was freed and pardoned, the Attorney, Sollicitor, Master of the Requests, and those that were acquainted with the Draught of the Petition, were all of them commanded to the Tower . . . And this was the end of our Law-sports, concerning the Night of Errors.

APPENDIX 2: PASSAGES FROM THE BIBLE

In the Introduction I have referred (pp. 10–11 above) to Shakespeare's extensive use of the Bible in the composition of *The Comedy of Errors*. I have quoted relevant passages from the Acts of the Apostles and a few short excerpts from the Epistle of St Paul to the Ephesians and other parts of the Bible. I here reproduce more fully, from the 1591 edition of the Bishops' Bible, the verses in Ephesians on which Shakespeare drew for important episodes in the play.

Ephesians 4, verses 22–4:

To lay downe according to the former conuersation, the old man, which is corrupt according to the lusts of errour: / To be renued in the spirite of your mind, / And to put on that new man, which after God is shapen in righteousnes, and holinesse of trueth.
    (Compare *The Comedy of Errors* 4.3.12–13)

Ephesians 5, verses 22–5, 28, 33:

Wiues, submit your selus vnto your owne husbands, as vnto the Lord: / For the husbande is the head of the wife, even as Christ is yᵉ head of the Church, and he is the sauiour of the body. / But as the Church is subiect vnto Christ, like wise the wiues of their owne husbands in all things. / Ye husbandes loue your wiues, even as Christ also loued the Church, and gaue himselfe for it, / . . . So ought men to loue their wiues, as their owne bodies: he that loueth his wife, loueth himselfe. / . . . Let every one of you loue his wife even as himselfe, and let the wife reuerence her husbande.
    (Compare *The Comedy of Errors* 2.1.7–25; 2.2.112–37)

Ephesians 6, verses 5, 9:

Seruants, obey them that are your bodily masters with feare and trembling, in singlenesse of your heart, as vnto Christ. / . . . And ye masters, do the same things vnto them, putting away threatnings: knowing that your master also is in heauen, neither is respect of person with him.
    (Compare *The Comedy of Errors* 2.2.26–34; 4.4.26–34)

Ephesians 6, verses 11–17:

Put on all the armour of God, that yee may stande against the assaults of the deuill. / For we wrestle not against blood and flesh, and against rulers, against powers, against worldly gouernours of the darknes of this world, against spirituall wickednesse in heavenly places, / Wherefore take vnto you the whole armour of God, that ye may bee able to resist in the euill day, and hauing finished all things, to stand fast. / Stand therefore, hauing your loynes girt about with the trueth, and hauing on the breast plate of righteousnesse; / And your feete shod in the preparation of the Gospel of peace. / Aboue all, taking the shielde of faith, wherewith ye may quench al the fiery darts of the wicked. / And take the helmet of saluation, and the sworde of the spirite, which is the worde of God.

(Compare various passages in *The Comedy of Errors*)

READING LIST

This list includes details of books and articles referred to in the Introduction or Commentary and may serve as a guide to those who wish to undertake further study of the play.

Alexander, Peter. *Shakespeare's Life and Art*, 1939
    Shakespeare, 1964
Arthos, J. 'Shakespeare's transformation of Plautus', *Comparative Drama* 1 (1967), 239–53
Baldwin, T. W. *William Shakspere Adapts a Hanging*, 1931
    William Shakspere's Small Latine and Lesse Greeke, 2 vols., 1944
    'Three homilies in *The Comedy of Errors*', in *Essays in Honor of Hardin Craig*, 1962
    On the Compositional Genetics of 'The Comedy of Errors', 1965
Barber, C. L. 'Shakespearean comedy in *Errors*', *College English* 25 (1964), 493–7
Barton, Anne. Introduction to *The Comedy of Errors* in Riverside
Bonazza, B. O. *Shakespeare's Early Comedies: A Structural Analysis*, 1966
Bradbrook, Muriel. *The Growth and Structure of Elizabethan Comedy*, 1955
Brown, J. R. *Shakespeare and his Comedies*, 1957
Cecil, Lord David. 'Shakespearean comedy', in *The Fine Art of Reading*, 1957, pp. 23–77
Champion, L. S. *The Evolution of Shakespeare's Comedy: A Study in Dramatic Perspective*, 1970
Charlton, H. B. *Shakespearian Comedy*, 1938
Clemen, W. H. *The Development of Shakespeare's Imagery*, 1951
Coghill, N. 'The basis of Shakespearian comedy', in *Essays and Studies* n.s. 3 (1950), 1–28
Curry, J. V. *Deception in Elizabethan Comedy*, 1955
Dent, R. W. *Shakespeare's Proverbial Language*, 1981
Doran, Madeleine. *Endeavors of Art*, 1954
Draper, J. W. 'Mistaken identity in Shakespeare's comedies', *Revue Anglo-Américaine* 11 (1933–4), 289–97
Elliott, G. R. 'Weirdness in Errors', *University of Toronto Quarterly* 9 (1939), 95–106
Evans, Bertrand. *Shakespeare's Comedies*, 1960
Fergusson, F. '*Errors* and *Ado*', *Sewanee Review* 62 (1954), 23–47; repr. in *The Human Image in Dramatic Literature*, 1957
Lerner, L. *Shakespeare's Comedies: An Anthology of Modern Criticism*, 1968
Muir, K. *Shakespeare: The Comedies. A Collection of Critical Essays*, 1965
Price, H. T. *Construction in Shakespeare*, 1951
Tillyard, E. M. W. *Shakespeare's Early Comedies*, 1956
Williams, S. '*Errors* rescued from tragedy', *Review of English Literature* 5 (October 1964), 63–71